✣ Keys to a Successful Retirement ✣

KEYS TO A
SUCCESSFUL
RETIREMENT

Staying Happy, Active, and Productive in Your Retired Years

FRITZ GILBERT

Illustrations by Lisa Quine

ROCKRIDGE
PRESS

Interior and Cover Designers: Matt Girard and Tricia Jang
Art Producer: Sue Bischofberger
Editor: Marisa A. Hines
Production Editor: Matthew Burnett

Illustrations © 2020 Lisa Quine

ISBN: Print 978-1-64611-339-2 | eBook 978-1-64611-340-8

R0

To my dad,
who gave me his writer's gene.

To my wife,
who gives me love.

To God,
who gives me life.

Contents

Introduction

You're standing on the cusp of a new horizon, a journey to a place you've never been. It's been a tough road to get here, and you should be proud for making it this far. As you start this book, allow me to offer you a sincere congratulations for a job well done. You've conquered many milestones as you've put yourself into the place where retirement is now a reality. You've paid attention to the financial side of things, saved as much as possible, and "paid yourself first" for decades.

You're ready to go.

The road ahead, however, is nothing like the road you've traveled thus far. You're likely a bit curious at this point about what lies ahead, perhaps even a bit apprehensive. I know that I certainly was. You know things are going to be different, but you don't really know how different they'll be. If I had to summarize the difference in one word, I'd choose … *freedom*.

A freedom unlike anything you've experienced since before you started school as a child. For most of your life you've had other people telling you what to do—your teacher, your coach, your boss. That stops now.

Welcome to a coffee break that will last for the rest of your life. In fact, that first cup of coffee on your first morning of retirement will be one of the best cups of coffee you've ever had in your life.

You're about to experience a new level of freedom that is both exhilarating and intimidating. A future that you have the freedom to shape. A future that can be anything you choose for it to be, along with the personal responsibility that comes with having to make that choice.

What do you want your life to be? That's a tough question to answer, and I'd be willing to bet you're going to be asking yourself that question many times over the days ahead. It's a question only you can answer, and it's an answer that will only happen if you make it happen.

You hold in your hands a roadmap for a journey that will last the rest of your lifetime. A roadmap to help you rest assured that you won't run out of money. More importantly, a roadmap to help you determine what you want to make of your retirement—and of your life. It's a map that's been drawn by the thousands of people who have walked this journey ahead of you. This journey is unlike any you've taken before and one that no one can understand until they've ridden a few miles down this strange new road. This book will help you navigate the curves ahead and help ensure that you'll enjoy the ride.

I've been writing about this journey every week for the past five years at The Retirement Manifesto, an online blog I founded to share my experience as I prepared for and transitioned into retirement. I've learned a lot through the experience and am excited to compile my most valuable learnings into this book. My goal is to provide some wisdom to smooth your transition, with the ultimate goal of helping people achieve a great retirement. As I do this, sometimes you will note that I include advice or situations originating from "we." For some, retirement is an individual undertaking. For others, it involves input and shared decision-making with a partner. My wife, Jackie, has been integral in my retirement journey, and as such, within this book I often include advice and examples that include more than simply my point of view.

To start, let me give you a glimpse of the first few curves you're going to face on this road called retirement. When you first leave the starting line, you're going to feel an exhilaration you haven't felt since that spring break in college when you and a carload of friends headed south to whatever beach was "in" that year. You've completed your exams, and you're FREE.

I recall like yesterday the smile that seemed to be frozen on my face for the first month of my retirement. "I don't have to go to work again, EVER!" was a common thought. The freedom of no alarm clock after decades of waking up at 5:30 a.m. to beat the morning commute into the city. Not only do I no longer have to deal with the alarm clock, I don't even have to deal with a commute!

For the first three to six months of retirement, you'll likely be knocking off a lot of items on a "to-do" list around the house. You'll still have that smile, and you'll be feeling some satisfaction at the things you're completing. However, this phase will eventually end. There are only so many things that need to be done around the house, and eventually you'll have completed the list.

At about the one-year mark, I want you to pull this book back off your shelf. (Go ahead and make a calendar entry now to remind yourself. I'll wait . . .) It's at that point in your retirement that the words you're about to read will become most important. It's hard to describe, but you'll know what I'm talking about when you take that turn in the road. There's a point in your retirement when you realize that this is your new reality. This is now your life. You'll likely get more introspective than you've been in a long time, and that's a good thing.

That's when I'm asking you to read this book again.

If you want to get the maximum benefit from this book, I'd offer the following suggestions:

- → Start applying some of the lessons in this book as you read them over the coming days.

- → Buy a notebook and start writing things down.

- → Buy a yellow highlighter and mark the heck out of this book as you read it the first time.

Enjoy that first cup of coffee on your first morning of retirement. You've certainly earned it. Most of the big ideas from this book will take a while to simmer. The longer you give them to simmer, the better that cup of coffee will taste.

Then, when you hit that sharp turn about a year up the road, come on back and have another look at the map you're currently holding in your hands. This map is the most I can offer to help you on your journey. The rest is up to you.

CHAPTER

1

Retirement Is Like Baking a Cake

> "Where there is cake, there is hope.
> And there is always cake."
>
> —Dean Koontz

Metaphors are interesting, and I've always appreciated their ability to help explain complex subjects. Perhaps I'm unique, but my brain somehow grasps onto concepts when they are presented through a metaphor. I hope your brain works in this way, too, because that's what I've decided to do with the first chapter of this book. I have assembled a metaphor that permeates most of the remaining pages of this book to help you understand and apply the concepts and ideas presented within.

Of primary importance is that this book is about the keys to a successful retirement. That is the point, and that is what matters. Since you've purchased this book, it's obviously a topic you care about. So, we seem to be off to a good start together.

With that as a background, I hope you enjoy reading concepts about retirement presented as metaphors because that's how we're going to start our time together.

Preparing for Retirement Is Like Baking a Cake

That seems like a simple sentence when you first read it. As you'll see in the coming pages, however, it's a metaphor that's rich in content (bad pun intended). Just as in baking a cake, retirement requires detailed planning, careful selection of what to include and what to omit, and a process to combine the elements into an end product you can enjoy for as long as it lasts.

If we do it right, baking this "retirement cake" together should be the perfect way to start your journey toward a great retirement. Let's get started ...

Planning Your Recipe

Back when I was working, our annual vacation was always a big priority for my family. Every year during our winter break, we'd spend a lot of time planning for our vacation the following summer. We enjoyed talking through various destination options and deciding where we were going to go. We'd spend hours online looking at gorgeous pictures of paradise before finalizing the plans for our much-anticipated summer vacation.

We always figured that since our vacation would only be one to two weeks, we might as well stretch the planning process as long as possible to get a little extra enjoyment from the anticipation of the big event. Rather than simply having two weeks to enjoy our vacation, we'd end up with a little carrot dangling in front of us for half a year. It kept vacations more exciting. It kept life more fun. Most importantly, it resulted in better vacations than if we'd waited until a few weeks before our departure to figure out what we were going to do.

When you're planning to bake a cake, you've got to do some work ahead of time. The reality is that you can't bake a cake until you decide what type of cake you'd like to create. Similarly, you shouldn't launch a retirement until you decide what type of life you'd like to live in your retirement years. It amazes me how some people can put less time into planning their retirement than they put into planning their annual vacation. Don't be one of those people.

≡ RETIREMENT TIP 1 ≡

Invest as much time as possible into planning for your retirement.

An *investment* is a commitment of a resource that generates future returns. The time you spend planning for your retirement is very much an investment, one that will pay back exceedingly high returns. You'll see numerous references to the importance of retirement planning over the course of this book. I've come to realize that retirement preparation is, perhaps, the single biggest key to a successful retirement.

When I was approximately three years away from retirement, I began researching what makes a great retirement. I was curious about what made the difference between a "good" versus a "bad" retirement. In over three decades of working, I'd seen plenty of people struggle with the transition. I was focused on doing everything possible to ensure the smoothest possible transition for my retirement. What I learned will also help you in your transition.

There is a direct correlation between the amount of time people invest in planning for their retirement and the resulting success of their subsequent life as a retiree. Those who invest the least amount of time tend to have a higher probability of experiencing the problems you typically hear about, such as boredom, loss of identity, and so on. Those who invest the most tend to have a much easier transition and higher satisfaction levels.

Typically, the hardest transitions are the hard-charging Type-A workaholics who work right up until their last day on the job. I've seen it firsthand, and I suspect you have, too. The problem is particularly acute when someone gets forced into retirement without seeing it coming. It's more common than most people realize, and I've dedicated some space to this issue later in this book.

The smoothest transitions are experienced by those who have invested the most amount of time in planning for their life of retirement. I'll admit, I was a bit nervous about how well my wife and I would handle the transition. I'd been a Type-A "Corporate Guy" for more than three decades, and I typically got restless on a long holiday weekend. Rather than simply worrying about the transition, I decided to do something about it.

Three years before my retirement, I started writing a blog about retirement. Every single week, for three straight years, I wrote about retirement. I thought about retirement more than anyone I know. It may have been bordering on obsessive, but it was something I really enjoyed. I figured I was only going to retire once, so why not spend as much time as possible learning about it before I entered the realm of the unknown? If there's nothing else you remember from this book, please *remember the importance of spending as much time as possible planning for your retirement.* The goal of the planning stage when baking a cake is to determine what type of cake you'd like to make so you can then implement the steps required to create your perfect cake. Similarly, the goal of retirement planning is to determine what type of life you want to create for yourself in retirement so you can then implement the steps required to create your perfect retirement.

The most important step in the process is *determining what type of life you want to live in your retirement years.* As you'll see, this drives the financial aspects of retirement and has a direct impact on when you'll be able to retire. More importantly, it also has a direct impact on what you decide to do in retirement, where you decide to do it, and what issues you'll prioritize in your life. If you don't yet know what type of retirement cake you're hoping to bake, I encourage you to make this the priority over the next few months of your life.

A few words are in order for those of you who are arriving late to the party. Perhaps you're on the eve of retirement and reading this book is the first step you've taken to prepare. Perhaps you've just gotten word from your employer that your days are numbered and you never saw it coming. Perhaps you're already retired and are now possibly feeling a bit lost and just now realize that you should have done some planning.

The very fact that you're reading this book is an encouraging sign, and I've little doubt you'll manage your transition well. The lack of planning doesn't automatically indicate you'll have a tough transition, but it means you've got to get serious about your retirement and you've got to get serious now. We'll talk in future chapters about some steps I recommend you consider taking. While some of the steps are more beneficial when given a longer amount of planning time, you'll benefit by taking the steps at any point in your retirement journey.

For starters, let me congratulate you on picking up this book. Please don't put it down without completing it. The really good stuff is reserved for the later chapters, even though you may think that the money chapter is the one that really matters. Bear with me and you'll find that, if your goal is to have a successful retirement, the money stuff doesn't matter nearly as much as you think it does. The real frosting for this cake is found in chapter 5, and no cake is complete without the frosting.

Finally, we've all had the experience of getting short notice for a dinner guest or a phone call that a friend just went into the hospital. No time to plan and no awareness that this was going to hit us today. Even with little to no planning, many a wonderful cake has been baked.

Gathering the Ingredients

If you've decided to create a vanilla cake, you don't have much use for cocoa. The type of cake you're planning to make has a direct impact on the ingredients required. The same principle applies to retirement.

As you work through the planning process, focus on the end product you're attempting to build. Put your energy into thinking about what you want your life to be like in retirement. The life you've chosen to build will dictate the ingredients required. If, for example, you want to travel across the United States, you'll need to think about an RV. If you want to travel around the world in luxury, you'd better ensure you have the financial means to pay for it.

Focus on the type of life you want to live
in retirement, and let that drive your list
of required ingredients.

Money is the number one ingredient people think about when they're first designing their retirement cake, for good reason. It's the one ingredient that you must have in sufficient quantity before baking your retirement cake. If you find out too late that you're short of this type of egg, you're going to have a hard time finding a neighbor who's willing to lend you a few to cover your needs. Money, therefore, is most often the ingredient that determines when you're able to retire.

How do you determine how much money you need for retirement? That's a question you've likely asked yourself numerous times over the past few years, and it's one you need to answer correctly. Books far larger than this one have been dedicated to answering that question. I'm committing chapter 2 to discussing some financial principles that will help you live a successful retirement. For the sake of this chapter, I'd like to focus on a simple formula that is critical to include in your retirement cake recipe. Using this formula will be helpful to ensure that you've gathered sufficient eggs to proceed with baking your cake.

In the simplest form, the amount of money you need to retire is an amount equal to 25 to 30 times the estimated annual spending requirements you expect to fund from your investments. If, for example, you expect to spend $50,000 per year and have no other income, you'd need $1.25 to $1.5 million of assets in place before you could realistically expect to retire:

$50,000 \times 25 = \$1,250,000$

$50,000 \times 30 = \$1,500,000$

An obvious question arises as you look at the approximately $1.5 million figure. How do you estimate the $50K of annual living expenses? As mentioned earlier, the retirement you decide to build will drive the ingredients. Live a life of luxury, and you'll obviously need more eggs. Live a life of frugality, and you can get by with fewer. We'll dig into this topic in chapter 2, but it's worth highlighting here as you think about the ingredients required.

Another retirement design question that will drive your required ingredients is whether you're planning on working in retirement and whether that work will generate some supplemental income. This is a significant question that only you can answer, but it's an important consideration that will drive a certain set of ingredients. If, for example, you'd like to pursue consulting in your retirement years, it's important to evaluate what you'll need to make that dream a reality. You'll want to take into consideration the potential need for a website, perhaps a blog to demonstrate your expertise, and a network that you'll maintain to generate potential consulting leads. The decision to work will also have an impact on the amount of money you'll need on hand before starting your retirement cake. I'd encourage you to be conservative in your assumptions, given the reality that your supplemental income may well be less than you expect it to be. Better to have too many eggs, rather than too few, as you're building your retirement cake.

While most people instinctively think of money as the most important ingredient for retirement, I've learned something interesting as I've made my transition into retirement. I'd heard others say, "You won't think much about money after you retire," but I didn't really believe it. However, it turns out that this phenomenon is very real and experienced by most people as they move through retirement.

As your retirement evolves, money becomes something you think about less and less. You know how much you have to spend, and you live your life accordingly. Over time, money becomes less important than it did during your accumulation years in the workplace. It may seem strange, but I've experienced it myself, and most retirees I've talked to have gone through a similar shift in priorities. I suspect you'll find, as I did, that nonfinancial ingredients become the real ingredients for a great retirement cake.

≡ RETIREMENT TIP 3 ≡

Spend time thinking about the nonfinancial ingredients of your retirement. In time, you'll find they're more valuable than money.

This book is dedicated to providing the keys to a successful retirement. I am convinced that you will come to find that the drivers of a truly successful retirement extend far beyond financial ingredients. Therefore, as we think about the ingredients required to make a truly satisfying retirement cake, I'd encourage you to keep the following major ingredients on hand:

ATTITUDE. If you go into retirement with a positive attitude, you'll increase your odds of an enjoyable journey. The inverse is also true. Fortunately, we can influence our attitude to a large degree. As you prepare for retirement, focus on having the right attitude. It's a critical ingredient to a great retirement.

CURIOSITY. Retirement is a time of freedom to explore your surroundings. Take advantage of your freedom and experiment with things that interest you. Look at things from a perspective of curiosity, and have fun trying things you've never tried before. Curiosity will lead you places you never saw coming, and you're likely to discover something that you become passionate about. Passion and purpose will be your keys to unlock a truly great retirement, the frosting on this cake. Pursue them relentlessly, and let curiosity guide your feet. Serendipity is my favorite word, for good reason.

GENEROSITY. For decades, you've been worrying about gathering resources to fund your retirement. The time has come to give back. Most people find that true contentment increases as you find ways to help others during your retirement. Go ahead and throw that expired jar of selfishness in the garbage, and make sure you've got an extra-large jar of generosity on hand as you begin to mix your cake. Even if money is tight, you can now afford to be generous with your time. Sprinkle some generosity in—it adds a marvelous flavor to your cake.

FOOD FOR YOUR MIND. Keeping your brain well fed is an important part of retirement. You'll lose the stimulation your workplace has historically provided, and it's up to you to replace it. As you buy the ingredients for your retirement cake, make sure you buy some food for your brain. Stock up on some good reading material, consider an online course in a topic of interest, sign up for a few e-mail lists to keep interesting things flowing into your inbox, etc. I've put together a list of recommended resources at the end of the book (see page 115), and I would encourage you to stack a few books in the kitchen as you compile your ingredients.

LIFESTYLE NEEDS. Beyond money, make sure you're thinking about what material goods need to be in place to live the retirement life you desire. Are you planning on downsizing in retirement or traveling the country in an RV? It's been proven that mixing your retirement lifestyle needs into the bowl early in the process helps improve your retirement experience. What do you need to live a life that will be fulfilling to you? Make a plan now for getting those ingredients in place at the right time.

SOCIAL CONNECTIONS. Life is more fun with others. Find a way to build new friendships and be intentional about maintaining social connections.

A TEAM OF EXPERTS. Retirement isn't a game. If you're uncomfortable with any of the aspects of retirement planning, build an appropriate team of experts. Don't be afraid to ask for help when you need it, and I'm not just referring to financial needs. Retirement is a time to reduce the stress in your life. If pulling in some experts helps you achieve this, then building these resources now should be a priority.

FITNESS. You're not getting any younger. If you don't start taking care of your body now, you'll likely regret it in a decade or so. Dedicate yourself to getting in shape with your newfound free time. Start with an easy walk three to five times per week. Consider other approaches to fitness as you gather your ingredients, such as a gym membership or exploring a hiking club in your area. Build this into your retirement lifestyle early, and let it bake into a beneficial habit for your retirement years.

SPIRITUALITY. Now that your working life is behind you, you'll have more time to be introspective. Take advantage of this freedom to think about your spirituality and what's deeply important in your life. To find true fulfillment in retirement, be honest with yourself about what role you want spirituality to play and focus on investing some time and energy in this aspect of your life.

Your list may look different than mine, but the point is this: Look far beyond financial considerations as you decide what ingredients you'll need on hand for your retirement. Many of the items included in the preceding list will be helpful regardless of what type of cake you're baking, and I'd encourage you to include a bit of each ingredient. Also, it's helpful to recognize that retirement is flexible, and there's nothing wrong with revisiting your list every few years to see if there are new ingredients that should be added or stale ingredients that you should discard. You're going to be working on this cake for a long time, so don't be in a hurry to get it done. Patience in the kitchen pays dividends in the dining room.

Layering Your Cake

When creating a cake, there's a certain sequence of steps that must be followed to achieve your desired end result. A recipe will typically start with a first step, which may require you to preheat the oven to a specific temperature and grease an eight-inch round baking pan.

While a great retirement may not be as simple as following a prescribed list of steps, there is a general process that has been proven to be helpful in achieving one.

FINANCES. As a first step, your focus will be on the finances, as mentioned earlier. Getting this part right is important, which is why I'm committing chapter 2 to the topic. It's the natural place to start and will be your primary focus for a while. As you're working through the numbers, remind yourself that figuring out the money is far from the only step required to create a great retirement.

ATTITUDE. As an important second step in your recipe, I'd encourage you to mix a big pinch of attitude into your bowl. There is nothing that will help you achieve a successful retirement more than having a positive attitude about it. Make a decision early in the process that you're going to approach retirement with optimism, curiosity, and gratitude. Of course, you're going to be apprehensive, but decide now that you'll focus on the positive and take steps to avoid the negative as you begin to build your retirement cake.

OPTIMAL TIMING. Consider your baking time as the time period between when your financial details are in place and when you're ready to spread some frosting. The time this cake needs to be in the oven will vary, but plan on it baking through your first year of retirement or so. While your cake is baking, dedicate yourself to pursuing the softer side of retirement. Take time to savor your transition, but realize it's only a small step in the process of creating a perfect cake. Enjoy your retirement dinner, and be introspective as you think about the years of your life you've committed to your work. Enjoy your work friendships in your final days while realizing they'll be different in the future. Recognize that you haven't finished baking your cake yet and you've only just started to think about the frosting.

PASSION. Creating the ultimate frosting is as much artistry as it is science, and the recipe will be uniquely yours. It's a custom blend of the softer stuff that matters most to you, resulting in a frosting that reflects and fulfills all of your dreams for retirement. It's finding a passion that connects you with others while fulfilling your deepest needs. Creating and spreading the perfect frosting is an art that will consume years of your life. It's the focus of chapter 5 in this book, and it's the basis of a truly spectacular retirement cake.

In closing, it's important to recognize that you'll be in this kitchen for the rest of your life. This retirement cake you're currently baking will never be entirely completed. The beauty of the process is that this is a cake you can change anytime you choose. Tired of vanilla and want to switch to chocolate? That decision is within your control.

Retirement is all about enjoying the present, so relax a bit. You've earned it. Your retirement cake is going to be in the oven for a while, so slow down and get comfortable. You've got a few years to figure out the frosting, and you want to give it the effort it deserves.

After all, isn't the frosting always the best part of the cake?

THINGS ARE DIFFERENT THESE DAYS

———◇———

I remember when I started my job in corporate America in 1985. There was a person who worked in my office named Junior who retired shortly after I joined the company. Junior encouraged me to stay with the company for my career, saying the pension and retiree medical plans were so generous that you could retire without really having saved much money. Junior was fortunate to be among the last of the retirees to reap the benefits of the golden era of pensions and retiree benefits.

Ironically, I was also encouraged by our HR group to sign up for our "new" 401(k) plan, launched in response to the Revenue Act of 1978, which enabled pretax employee contributions to retirement plans. Like most companies, the rollout of the 401(k) was the first in a series of steps that had far-reaching consequences for retirees. In time, companies realized that a "defined contribution" plan like a 401(k) was a less problematic obligation than a "defined benefit" plan such as a traditional pension. By definition, "defined benefit" plans required companies to pay a specific benefit to participants regardless of market performance. Companies had to increase funding in times of poor performance to maintain a legally required pension funding level. Contrast this with "defined contribution," in which the only obligation was to contribute a defined amount. The participant had no guarantee of performance and future benefit, and the employer avoided the obligation of delivering a guaranteed future benefit. As a result, the number of private sector companies offering "defined benefit" pensions has dropped to 17 percent, compared with 62 percent in 1983. In contrast, 71 percent of companies now offer "defined contribution" plans like a 401(k). The burden for retirement planning has clearly shifted from employer to employee.

After the 2010 passage of the Affordable Care Act (ACA), my employer and many others dropped retiree health care coverage, which had long been a standard benefit for retirees. Prior to this bill, many employers felt an obligation to provide health insurance to their retirees due to the moral dilemma of having retirees potentially unable to secure insurance due to preexisting conditions. When the ACA eliminated this obstacle, retiree medical insurance was quickly dropped by the majority of companies, and retirees were forced to navigate the treacherous waters of the private health insurance market alone.

With the reduction of retiree benefits and employers' willingness to quickly downsize workforces based on market demand, loyalty between employer and employee has been severely impacted. While employers previously had the "golden handcuffs" of a rich pension plan, today's employee is free to move about with no repercussions to their longer-term retirement benefits.

While I started my career with Junior citing the benefits of lifelong service to one employer, I ended it with today's Millennials passing through the company so quickly I could scarcely keep track of any of them. I remember watching one individual quit after 18 months in a job, deciding he'd rather travel around Latin America for a year with his wife before they settled down to start a family. He was 26 years old. A year later, he returned to the area and got a decent job with another employer without missing a beat. "Mini-retirements" are now an option, regardless of one's age.

Looking back through the changes from the beginning to the end of my career, it's hard to determine which system was "better." Both had advantages and disadvantages. Macro forces will continue to drive change that is far beyond our ability to control. It's possible we'll see serious changes to the American system of Social Security within our lifetimes as well as increasing pressure on governments to provide promised benefits to tomorrow's retirees. The only thing constant is change, and we would be naive to think that's going to change anytime soon.

The best we can do is create the best retirement cake we can from the ingredients that we have on hand or can reasonably collect.

CHAPTER

2

What to Do When the Paycheck Stops

> *"Retirement is wonderful if you have two essentials—much to live on and much to live for."*
>
> —Author Unknown

There are few things in life more stressful than realizing your paycheck is stopping, forever. The transition from decades of accumulating wealth to the start of withdrawing from your portfolio can cause significant anxiety as you move into retirement. Many experts break retirement planning and operationalization into two phases: accumulation and withdrawal. This chapter is focused on discussing the approach we've used in our retirement to successfully manage the "withdrawal phase," with the hope that you'll discover a method that reduces the financial anxiety you may have around retirement.

In time, I suspect you'll find that money isn't what drives true happiness in retirement. That statement seems counterintuitive, but everyone I've talked to who has spent time in retirement reaches the point when they think less about money and more about the things that truly provide meaning to their retirement years. Regardless, as you prepare for retirement, you're likely worried about your financial situation, so let's address it.

Establishing a firm financial foundation is tremendously helpful in allowing you to pursue the things that provide meaning to you in the years ahead. Concerns about money need to be addressed as one of the keys to a successful retirement, so I've outlined this chapter using the methodology that worked well for my wife and me. We no longer worry about money, and we have in place an easy-to-manage process that replicates a regular paycheck flowing into our checking account. I don't know if it'll be right for you, but it's worth sharing. We'll start with the fundamentals, after which I'll outline our specific "retirement paycheck" approach.

To begin, there are at least three key financial areas that should be addressed in your retirement-planning stage:

1. *Do I have enough money to retire?*

2. *How much can I spend in retirement?*

3. *What do I do when the paycheck stops?*

First, a brief disclaimer. I'm writing from the perspective of a person who has focused intently on the topic of retirement for the past five years. I'm a "passionate personal financial hobbyist," but I am NOT a licensed financial professional. My advice comes strictly from my experience, and my situation is not the same as yours. No one should read these words and blindly adopt them. If you're not comfortable addressing the financial specifics of your retirement, hire someone who is an expert (see Retirement Resources, page 115, for more details).

Deciding when you will retire and how you'll handle financial issues in retirement is the most important financial decision you'll make in life. Consider my words those of an individual who has made a successful transition into retirement, not as specific recommendations for your own situation.

For your entire career, you've been accumulating assets to support your eventual retirement. That retirement has now arrived, and you'll undergo a significant shift as you begin to withdraw those assets to fund your retirement. I'll explain the system we've set up for our withdrawals and encourage you to establish a system that works for you in order to minimize worry as you begin spending your assets. My hope is that this chapter will provide suggestions from which you can form a system that minimizes your money worries, allowing you to get on with the task of enjoying your retirement.

How Much Can You Spend in Retirement?

The question of how much you can spend in retirement is directly linked to when you'll be able to retire. The more you'd like to spend, the more you'll need to have saved before you're able to retire. Spend less, and you'll need less saved. Seems obvious. The more challenging question is how you go about determining if you're able to retire now . . .

⇒ . . . with the amount of money you'd like to spend.

⇒ . . . with the resources you currently have saved.

Three years prior to my retirement, my wife and I decided to get serious about determining when I would be able to retire. We spent a lot of time talking through what we wanted our retirement to be and how much it would cost. The steps we followed answered the preceding questions, and the process we used worked well for us. If you're married or planning on retiring with a significant other, I encourage you to consider going through the following exercise together. It's important to incorporate each of your desires into the design of your retirement. With that, here's how my wife and I went about planning for the day my paycheck would stop.

First, we got serious about tracking our spending. I know, the very thought of that is enough to make you skip this chapter. Bear with me, this is important stuff—I'd encourage you to read this entire chapter before deciding how you'll build your financial foundation.

For one year, we tracked every dollar spent, manually, in a spreadsheet. I put receipts in my pocket whenever we spent money and updated my spreadsheet several times a week. It was tedious, but the resulting information was invaluable. For the first time in our lives, we had a 100 percent accurate baseline on how much money it took to live our lives, broken into spending categories. Step one: complete.

Second, we thought about how our spending would change in retirement. This is the most important step in the process, since it's here that you begin to build the foundation for the life you want to live in retirement. Think carefully about the retirement you want to live and how much it will cost. Focus on the lifestyle you desire first, and then get realistic about the costs associated with that lifestyle.

═ RETIREMENT TIP 4 ═

Track your actual preretirement
spending for a year, and then make
adjustments based on your retirement
lifestyle goals to get a firm estimate of
your retirement spending requirements.

As my wife and I planned for the type of retirement cake we wanted to bake, we incorporated as many of our lifestyle choices into our projected spending requirements as possible. For example, we wanted to travel cross-country in an RV, so we added a line in our budget for camping ($40/night × 100 nights/year = $4K of new camping spending for retirement). We carved out the money to buy the RV before we retired and adjusted our "starting cash position" by that amount.

We also knew we wanted to downsize to a cabin in the mountains, which we'd pay off when we sold our "city house" as part of our plan. We would become 100 percent debt-free in the process and no longer have a mortgage to pay in retirement. We also adjusted our estimated property taxes and utilities to reflect the lower costs associated with the cabin.

We ended up with an estimated "postretirement" spending requirement that was based on the life we envisioned living. This is the best way I'm aware of to determine how many eggs you need to make your retirement cake, and I'd encourage you to spend some time on this exercise.

Be realistic as you modify your "preretirement" spending to reflect your "postretirement" spending. Two areas where I'd warn you to pay special attention are:

→ Health care

→ Taxes

Since I retired at age 55, I'd have to pay for 10 years of private insurance before becoming eligible for Medicare. To be safe, I assumed a cost of $2,500/month, which I inflated at 5 percent per year. Yes, that's a lot of eggs, but I wanted to be sure that there were sufficient savings in place to cover this expense before taking the plunge into retirement. I researched the estimated costs of private health insurance and increased my estimates to build in a "fudge factor" for any unplanned surprises.

Regarding taxes, don't forget to factor in the reality that any pretax money you have sitting in a 401(k) or IRA is not entirely yours to spend. The tax obligation to access that money is an expense you need to bear in retirement, yet many people underestimate the significant cost of accessing before-tax investments. Don't make the mistake of assuming you can cover after-tax expenses with before-tax money. Include a specific line item to capture your estimated tax burden when withdrawing the before-tax money.

Whether you do it yourself or hire a professional to do it, make sure you've thought through the appropriate level of detail on tax expenses and included them in your analysis. In the Retirement Resources section (see page 115), you will find a variety of books as well as a few of my favorite retirement blogs that cover this topic. Spend time educating yourself on these issues as you're preparing.

Once you have your estimated retirement spending, the calculation to determine how much money you need is relatively straightforward. First, you need to determine how much income you will receive in retirement, including Social Security, pensions, part-time work, etc., and subtract that amount from your spending.

The goal is to determine how much of your annual spending you'll be covering from your savings. Once you've determined the annual spending from savings, you simply multiply that amount by 25 to 33 to determine a range of total savings required. The range will show a lower, more aggressive total with the 25x factor and a higher, more conservative total with the 33x factor.

Summarized, the formula to determine your total investments required is as follows:

1. *Spending Requirements – Income in Retirement = Annual Spending from Savings*

2. *Annual Spending from Savings × 25 to 33 = Range of Investments Required*

Here's a quick example:

1. *$80,000 Spending - $30,000 Social Security = $50,000 Annual Spending from Savings*

2. *$50,000 Annual Spending × 25 to 33 = $1.25 to $1.65 Million Investments Required*

In the example, you'll be able to spend $80K in your first year and you'll need a minimum of $1.25 million eggs on hand before you start mixing your retirement cake (or $1.65 million if you'd prefer to be more conservative). If you only have $1 million saved, you can conclude that you are not yet able to retire at the $80K spending level. As stated earlier, the type of cake you've decided to bake has a direct influence on the ingredients required. The larger your spending, the larger your required basket of eggs. The spending requirements should be based on the retirement life you're creating for yourself.

The 25x to 33x range that is used in the preceding formulas is based on a concept called "safe withdrawal rate," or SWR (also referred to as "sustainable withdrawal rate"). A 1998 study titled "Retirement Savings: Choosing a Withdrawal Rate That Is Sustainable," conducted at Trinity University, is seen as one of the most influential studies on safe withdrawal rates. The study, commonly referred to as "The Trinity Study," determined that a retiree can withdraw 4 percent of their nest egg in year one of their retirement, increasing each year by inflation. You'll notice in the example that $50K is 4 percent of $1.25 million, which was the total savings required using the 25x factor. Recent studies have recommended an SWR closer to 3 percent, which equates to the 33x factor ($50K = 3% of $1.65M). Further recommended reading is included in the Retirement Resources (see page 115) if you'd like to dig deeper into this topic. For this example, I've included both the 3 percent (33x) and 4 percent (25x) SWR in the calculation to show the range of required savings.

For people who have been forced into retirement, the equation is slightly different. In that situation, the number of eggs you have is a known figure, and you need to design a lifestyle that you'll be able to support with the ingredients you have on hand. In that case, you simply reverse the formula to determine how much you can spend in a year.

If, for example, you've been forced into retirement and you have $1 million in savings and expect $25,000 in Social Security, the answer to "how much can you spend in retirement" is calculated as follows:

$1M Portfolio × 4% SWR = $40K Investment Spending + $25K SS = $65K Annual Spending

$1M Portfolio × 3% SWR = $30K Investment Spending + $25K SS = $55K Annual Spending

In your first year of retirement, you can spend $65K, assuming a 4 percent SWR, or $55K if you're more conservative and go with a 3 percent SWR. Each year, you can increase your spending by the rate of inflation, and your money should last for the rest of your life. For example, if inflation runs at 3 percent in year one, you could increase your $65K by 3 percent for year two, an increase of $1,950 to a total of $66,950.

Since, in this example, you were forced into retirement, you will have to find a way to live within those limits. Alternatively, you could decide that you're unwilling to live at that level and go back to work to cover your living expenses and continue to grow your investments. Deciding to continue to work in retirement, even if only part-time, can have a dramatic impact on your withdrawal rate and should be a serious consideration if you're uncomfortable with the results of your calculation. In the example, if you're able to earn $20K through part-time work, you could increase your spending from $75K to $85K while still only withdrawing a "safe" $30K to $40K from investments.

Now, let's do the exercise for a $500K portfolio. How much can you spend assuming the same $25K in Social Security? If you answered $40K to $45K, you've passed the test. Now, try it with your actual numbers.

Creating a Retirement Paycheck

Now that you know how much you can spend in retirement, how do you set up a system to ensure you're spending what you're allowed to spend? One approach would be to develop a detailed budget and track what you're spending each month against your budgeted amount.

Personally, I'm not a fan of budgets. I didn't want to spend my retirement tracking my spending at that level of detail, and I know it isn't a system I would maintain. Tracking our actual spending for a year was difficult, and I didn't want to spend the rest of my life being obligated to do it. If budgeting works for you, knock yourself out. I decided to develop an easier method.

As I thought about how we managed our money throughout my career, I realized we never budgeted during my working years. We simply "paid ourselves first" by automatically investing into our 401(k) and automatic transfers to mutual funds. We knew we were saving aggressively and were free to spend whatever was left in our checking account. I decided to replicate this process for our retirement spending.

To start, I built up a cash reserve in a money market account equal to three years of our projected spending. Rather than share our exact figures, I'll use the first example in this chapter to explain our methodology. Recall these details from the example:

→ Annual Spending = $80,000

→ Social Security = $30,000

→ Spending from Investments = $50,000

We don't want to spend more than $50K from our portfolio of $1.5M, which reflects a 3.3 percent SWR. The first step was to build up a $150K balance of cash in our money market account, which equals $50K of annual investment spending times three years. It's important to build up this cash bucket prior to your retirement date to ensure that you have enough money set aside on day one to last for two to three years.

≡ RETIREMENT TIP 5 ≡

Build up cash reserves equal to two to three years of your spending prior to reaching retirement. This is the pool of cash you'll use to establish your retirement paycheck.

A note about the two-to-three-year cash target. A risk you'll face in retirement is called "sequence-of-returns risk," which is the risk of having to sell stocks during a bear market (defined as a stock market decline of 20 percent or more). If you have $1M entirely in stocks and the market goes down by 50 percent, you'd only have $500,000 in investments. The worst thing you can do is to sell $50K of stocks at this point, which would equate to a 10 percent withdrawal rate, leaving fewer stocks in your portfolio for the eventual market recovery. By building the cash cushion of $150K, you'd be able to withdraw $50K for three years without selling any stocks during the bear market. The length of your cash cushion should be based on your risk tolerance. We chose three years as a conservative approach, which would allow stocks three years after a bear market to rebound before we'd have to sell any stocks. Some would argue we're giving up potential investment returns by subjecting $150K to the meager returns of cash, but the avoidance of sequence-of-returns risk is worth it to us. You'll have to decide what risk tolerance level you're comfortable with and build your cash bucket accordingly.

As we started retirement, I established an automatic monthly transfer from our money market account to our checking account. To determine the amount, you simply divide the $50K of annual spending by 12 months ($50K/12 months = $4,167). Once it's set up, you'll have a "paycheck" each month and you'll be free to spend whatever money is in your checking account.

A word about irregular, but not unexpected, expenses. Let's say your furnace dies and you're on the hook for a $5K furnace replacement or your car dies and you're suddenly looking at $30K to replace your car. What is the best way to handle this? In our case, we set aside $12K in an "emergency spending" account, to which we'll add $12K every year. I calculated the $12K by looking at what unplanned expenses should be expected. For example, if you expect a $5K furnace to last 15 years, you'd calculate $5K/15 years = $333 per year. A $30K car, driven for 10 years with a $10K residual value, would be $2K per year ($20K/10 years). We have two cars, so that's $4K per year. We included all major appliances and longer-term maintenance items (e.g., roof replacement at 15 years) and came up with a total of $12K per year.

We included our $12K in our withdrawal rate calculation and reduced our monthly paycheck by that amount (in the preceding example, the $50K would drop by $12K to $38K, which would then be subdivided into a monthly paycheck of $3,167).

Now, we can still spend whatever money we have in our checking account and know we can tap into the $12K reserve for any unplanned (but not unexpected) expenses without exceeding our SWR. Each year we'll add $12K to the reserve, and we'll have money set aside to buy that car for cash when it needs to be replaced or replace the furnace or the roof and so on. It adds a bit of complexity, but we like the assurance of knowing we've built in a buffer for the "surprise" expenses, which we all know are a reality in life.

On top of this $150K of cash reserves, we have two additional "buckets" of funds based on how far into the future we expect to require the funds. In total, then, we have three buckets, as follows:

→ **Bucket 1:** $150K, or 3 years × $50K, in cash or cash equivalents

→ **Bucket 2:** $250K to $350K, or 5 to 7 years, in bonds, CDs, REITs (some volatility, higher growth)

→ **Bucket 3:** $1M to $1.1M remainder in a stock portfolio (higher volatility, higher growth)

Theoretically, we could tolerate eight to 10 years in an extended bear market without selling any stocks (three years by using the cash and another five to seven years by selling the bonds). Note that the resulting asset allocation of the portfolio would be:

→ **Cash:** $150K, or **10 percent** of the $1.5M portfolio

→ **Bonds:** $250K–$350K, or ~**20 percent** of the $1.5M portfolio

→ **Stocks:** $1M–$1.1M, or ~**70 percent** of the $1.5M portfolio

In our case, we hold approximately 60 percent equity/ 40 percent cash and bonds, reflecting our more conservative approach. Your asset allocation is a critical element of your planning, and you should be intentional in setting a target based on your personal risk tolerance. Remember that inflation is also a risk in retirement, and try to maintain enough exposure to stocks to capture the higher growth rate required to mitigate the inflation risk.

≡ RETIREMENT TIP 6 ≡

Consider setting up a "bucket system,"
whereby you allocate investments
to one of three buckets based on
how long it will be before you need
to tap into the money.

As we spend down Bucket 1, we periodically "refill" it by selling stocks and bonds from Buckets 2 and 3, depending on how the markets are performing. If the markets are doing well, we refill Bucket 1 at least twice a year, maintaining as close to the three-year "full" level as possible.

If a bear market attacks, we'll pull several years from Bucket 1 without refilling, if necessary. This prevents selling stocks during the bear market. We'd also reduce spending a bit given the decline in our overall portfolio. We've built a cushion of "wants" into our budget, which could be eliminated with minimal sacrifice if necessary. We'd also look at selling some assets in Bucket 2 that haven't declined as severely as stocks to maintain at least a one-year buffer in Bucket 1.

If I've lost you at this point, don't wing it. Read through this section a few times and work out your numbers. If you're uncomfortable, hire a professional financial planner to work through your numbers and develop an approach that works for you.

The Impact of Housing on Your Spending Requirements

There are several important areas you should consider as you develop your spending needs for retirement. All of these lifestyle considerations have significant financial impact, so I've elected to include them in this chapter.

First, think about where you want to live and what type of house will meet your retirement dreams. The impact of this decision will have a material impact on your spending. It's important to decide this as you're calculating your estimated retirement spending.

If you're worried about the spending levels you've calculated, I encourage you to consider downsizing as part of your strategy. If you're empty nesters, you have less need for the space you required when raising a family. That empty space costs a lot of money, and it may be money you'd rather not spend on rooms you no longer use. A larger house also means more housework, something you may prefer to minimize in retirement.

If you're experiencing health issues, is now the time to move to a more accessible home while you still have enough mobility to handle the move? If your children have moved away, is there a lower-cost area that appeals to you? If you're in a high-tax state, have you considered relocating to a lower-tax state? Perhaps there's an area closer to your kids that you're considering? Build in some time to rent a house via Airbnb in a few different areas and live as a local for a few weeks to get a real feel for the area.

☰ RETIREMENT TIP 7 ☰

If you're planning to downsize
or relocate in retirement, spend
extended time in your new location
before you finalize your decision.
Get involved in your new community
while you're still working.

Seven years before retiring, my wife and I purchased a vacation cabin in the Appalachian Mountains. It was two hours away from our city home, and we used it for weekend getaways and longer stays during our vacations. When we weren't using it, we rented it out. The rental income covered the expenses of the second home, and it provided us an opportunity to fully evaluate the town where we now live. We made new friends in the area while we were still working and got involved in local charities on the weekends—important stuff, all of which we'll discuss more in coming chapters. Also, the sale of our "big house" in the city freed up home equity value that we used to pay off the mortgage on our retirement cabin. We became 100 percent debt-free and even had some excess home equity funds that we applied to our Bucket 1 cash reserves.

If you decide to downsize or relocate, consider when you'll make the move. Some people prefer to tackle the move after they have more time in retirement. No problem with that, but make sure you've thought through the cash-flow implications of potentially paying for two homes as you buy and sell the homes. Also realize that you'll be leaving your home base shortly after retirement, which may make for a more difficult transition to the new retirement area. There are pros and cons of moving sooner versus later, and I encourage you to think through the details with your spouse or partner as you finalize your plans.

A brief word on international relocations for retirement is in order. There is a growing trend of moving to lower-cost countries to reduce your spending in retirement. If this appeals to you, be realistic with your expectations. Do a lot of research and plan extended trips to your target country prior to your retirement. When you visit, don't travel as a tourist. Rather, look at renting a home for a few weeks that is comparable to what you'd expect to live in as a retiree. Connect with expats who have moved before you and discuss their honest experiences. Consider the legal requirements of living in a foreign country, and do your due diligence before you finalize your decision. For many people, spending a few years in a low-cost country adds some adventure to their retirement while reducing expenses. I have a friend, Jim, who retired in his 40s and is now enjoying retired life in Panama. (You can check out the details of his story at RouteToRetire.com.) It's too extreme a move for my wife and me, but it may be right for you. Make sure you've built a contingency plan in the event the move doesn't work out, and run the numbers for a worst-case scenario of moving back to the United States sooner than expected.

Another major consideration is whether you're planning on buying any "toys" for retirement. Your desired retirement lifestyle likely includes some toys, and there's nothing wrong with that. Just be aware that toys can be expensive, and include them in your financial calculations.

In our case, our toys included a new RV, a truck to pull it, two kayaks, and two bikes. We estimated the cost of each and made the decision to purchase the items before our retirement. We had a targeted "starting cash level" equal to three years of spending (Bucket 1, remember?) and made sure that we included the approximately $100K of toy spending in our calculations. Using the preceding example, we now needed $150K cash (3 years x $50K) plus $100K to buy our toys. Had we not done this, we could have spent the $100K on toys and ended up below target in our cash bucket on day one of retirement. In the final year of work, we reduced our contributions to savings and redirected the money into cash to help cover the required spending. We sold some stocks and used the reduced investment portfolio as our projected starting level for our SWR calculations. We also applied the excess home equity from the sale of our city house toward our cash-building exercise.

Finally, we decided to remodel the kitchen in our cabin before we retired. We met with various contractors and built in the estimated costs in the same manner we had used for the "toy" expenses. Once we had enough funds in place, we bought the toys and completed the remodel while also building a $150K Bucket 1 cash balance before we retired.

If you're going to do a major remodeling project or buy some toys, consider doing it while you're still working. Build them into your plans, and make sure you're taking steps to raise the required liquidity before you retire.

≡ RETIREMENT TIP 8 ≡

Plan to do any major spending required
to create your ideal retirement while
you're still working.

Making these expenditures before the paychecks stop flowing is helpful. Once those paychecks stop, it's more difficult to part with your eggs. You'll be more concerned about your finite resources, especially early in your retirement. Research has shown that those who are enjoying happy retirements tend to make their major expenditures prior to their retirement date.

Also, completing your targeted "toy spending" prior to retirement ensures that you'll start retirement with the appropriate level of cash on hand. If you overspend on toys and find yourself below your targeted cash level, you can continue working for the time required to build your cash back up to the targeted level. If you wait until you retire to buy the toys, any overspending can put you in the dangerous position of having insufficient cash on hand early in retirement, increasing your exposure to sequence-of-returns risk.

To continue the baking metaphor from the previous chapter, the aforementioned steps are intended to ensure you have sufficient eggs on hand before you start mixing your retirement cake. Be careful when spending those eggs on toys, but also remember that those toys are an important element in your recipe. Don't retire until you have Bucket 1 fully funded and have enough cash on hand to avoid selling stocks in a bear market. The worst thing you can do is start baking your retirement cake only to find out after you've left your job that you don't have enough eggs in your kitchen to complete your recipe.

DO YOU HAVE TOO MUCH PRETAX SAVINGS?

---◦---

If you're like me, you were encouraged to invest heavily in pretax vehicles during your career. When Baby Boomers were entering the workforce, IRAs and 401(k)s were just being introduced, and people quickly learned that the "before-tax" (pretax) option had appealing tax benefits. Any pretax contributions were deducted from your income for tax purposes, reducing your tax bill for the year in which you made the contribution. All earnings were also "tax deferred"—what a bonus! We knew the taxes would be due at some point in the far future, but we could deal with that later.

"Later" has now arrived. Uncle Sam isn't as generous as we may have been led to believe. He wants his taxes on that income you earned all those years ago, and he wants it now. In fact, if you don't start withdrawing your pretax contributions by the time you've reached age 72, he's going to make you do it through those nasty required minimum distributions (RMDs). RMDs are based on a formula dictated by the IRS, which requires you to pull an increasing percentage of your before-tax IRA/401(k) investments every year. As you withdraw those funds, you're going to have

to pay income taxes on the money. A quick note on age 72: With the passage of the new SECURE Act in late 2019, the age for RMDs was increased from 70½ to 72.

RMDs are catching some of the early wave of Baby Boomers by unpleasant surprise. They've reached that magical age of 72, and RMDs are now being forced upon them. They're facing a painful reality. Those taxes can really hurt, and it appears there's little that can be done to avoid them.

Don't wait until age 72 to manage your pretax contributions. There is a better way.

Don't wait until RMDs kick in at age
72 to manage your pretax retirement
savings. Consider "topping off" your tax
bracket each year with withdrawals from
your before-tax IRAs.

Any withdrawals from your pretax accounts are taxed at your marginal tax rate at the time of withdrawal. If you're pulling Social Security and a pension, it's possible those RMDs will push you into a higher tax bracket, resulting in higher taxes than desired. To minimize this risk, consider using the years between now and age 72 to withdraw a portion of your before-tax monies every year to "top off" your current tax bracket.

The following example helps clarify this strategy. Though tax brackets continually change, I will use the tax rates in effect for a married couple filing jointly during 2019. Any income between $19,400 and $78,950 is taxed at a rate of 22 percent. If your income is $50,000, you could withdraw $28,950 from your before-tax account while staying within the 22 percent tax bracket. "Topping off" describes the act of achieving the $78,950 income level via pretax withdrawals ($50K + $28,959), which represents the "top" of your current bracket.

If you choose not to do this, your tax rate could be higher when RMDs kick in. For example, if you're age 73 and your RMD forces you to withdraw $50K on top of your $50K of income, your total income of $100K will push you into the next higher tax bracket, resulting in a tax of 24 percent for the amount of the RMD that exceeds the $78,950 "top" of the 22 percent bracket.

It's a strategy we're using now, even though we're only in our mid-50s. We did our first withdrawal from our before-tax 401(k) last year, executing a rollover into a Roth account (that particular topic's beyond the scope of this chapter). It's important that you understand all the implications before you implement this strategy, such as potentially losing any ACA or Medicare subsidies you may qualify for with a lower income. Talk to your CPA or a certified financial planner, but it's a strategy you should consider if you're interested in minimizing your taxes in retirement.

CHAPTER 3

It's a New Day: Routines and Relationships

> "Retirement is like being out of school for
> the summer, but the summer never ends."
>
> —Author Unknown

While I was still working, I was intrigued about what life in retirement was really like. I remember asking several of my friends who had already retired what it was like to live life in retirement, but I was never fully satisfied with their answers. "Six days of Saturdays, every week" was a common sentiment. "A vacation that never ends" was another. But I knew there was so much more, and I had a strong yearning to experience the reality of that freedom.

As I came closer to my retirement date, I spent an inordinate amount of time thinking about the topic. Life in retirement is an interesting concept. It's something that none of us can ever fully understand until we live it ourselves. No matter how well someone explains it to you, you simply cannot fully relate until you've experienced it firsthand. Even if someone were able to describe it perfectly and you were able to grasp their explanation as they gave it, the reality is that no two people have the same experience in retirement. No two people go through the same transition.

I tried to extrapolate the feeling of a vacation to my everyday life but knew it wasn't a fair reflection of retirement reality. Try as I might, there was simply no way to anticipate what it was really going to be like. It was an interesting curiosity, and I've often wondered if I was alone in my fascination with the topic. I hope not, because that's what I've chosen to address in this chapter.

You're somewhere close to retirement and interested in what it's all about. After the obsession I had on the topic, how could I possibly write a book without attempting to address the strange fascination of what life in retirement is really like?

I find myself in the shoes of those friends I asked, and I'm wondering how best to describe it to you. I wish I could say "six days of Saturday, every week" or "a vacation that never ends," but we both know that's insufficient to a degree I can't even begin to explain.

Life in retirement is unlike anything you've ever experienced in your life. It's amazing, confusing, fun, unique, variable, flexible, mischievous, exciting, surprising, perplexing, bewildering, and so many other adjectives that I could easily make this the longest run-on sentence in the book. And yet even that doesn't explain what it's really like. Let's take a closer look at what retirement is . . . and what it isn't.

A New Day in an Empty Room

The possibilities in any given day are endless.

Dwell on that for a minute. Think about a Saturday in your current life, a day in which your possibilities are, indeed, endless. But the endless possibilities of a life in retirement are about SO much more than the possibilities of one Saturday per week. Your possibility for today is endless. Your possibility for tomorrow is endless. Next week. Next month. Next year. Endless possibilities, every day, for the rest of your life. Indeed, so much bigger than "just" a Saturday, but it's a start. Let's build on that foundation.

Imagine a closed door in front of you. The door is white. There's no window in the door, and there are no markings of any kind. The door is locked. On your retirement day, you're given the key to that door. You turn the key, feeling the apprehension build inside of you, and push open that door. Beyond the door is a white room that stretches to the horizon for as far as you can see, in all directions.

And you have a box of crayons. There are endless possibilities in this white room where you own crayons.

Now, imagine that anything you draw becomes a reality. You draw a lake on the floor, and suddenly you're swimming. You draw a mountain, and you're climbing. A sailboat, and you're sailing. A horse, and you're riding. Fun activities all, but don't limit yourself. Remember, these are the days of endless possibilities.

Go bigger.

Start thinking about the frosting on that retirement cake. Draw a person in need, and you're helping. A business owner who's struggling, and you're advising. A parentless orphan, and you're loving. A homeless dog, and you're rescuing. An addict, and you're counseling.

Are you getting the idea? Endless. Possibilities.

A new day in an empty room, indeed. A day unlike any you've ever experienced. One after another, after another, after another, after another. For the rest of your life.

It's time to start drawing.

═ RETIREMENT TIP 10 ═

Take the time in your final weeks of work to say goodbye to your true friends at work. Your relationships will change after retirement.

At 8:00 a.m. on Friday, I was packed up and heading down to the lobby, just like I'd done thousands of times in hotels throughout the world over the previous decades. I met a few of my coworkers by the front desk, and we jumped into a cab for our trip out to O'Hare Airport. Everything seemed so normal.

Except nothing seemed normal at all.

I remember exiting the plane in Atlanta and meeting up with my coworkers in the terminal just inside our arrival gate. We all realized the significance of the moment as we said farewell and took a photo together to memorialize my last minute as a citizen of corporate America. As I got in my truck and headed north, away from the city and toward our retirement cabin in the mountains, I realized it was really over. I was retired, and tomorrow would be my first day as a member of the retired class. I had officially crossed The Starting Line.

A new day had begun. A day in which work was optional, a day in which freedom was complete. Life would never be the same again.

The weekend felt, in many ways, like any other weekend. The biggest exception was the realization that my Monday morning commute would never arrive and the knowledge that I was officially retired. And yet it was still a Saturday morning, with a relaxing cup of coffee with my wife, sitting on the deck of our cabin looking out at the woods. It was familiar and yet entirely new. Not having the urge to check my e-mails wasn't a natural feeling, but it felt good—so, so good.

I smiled a lot that first weekend, that first week, that first month. I savored the reality that I would never again have to work. It's strange how that thought would pop into my mind at the most random of times and how a smile would form on my face whenever I thought it. People would have thought me nuts had they seen the random smile, at random times, for days on end. "So, this is what freedom feels like," I thought. "This is what it's like to be retired." Another smile.

I didn't set an alarm clock for four months. I quickly learned that one of my favorite times of the day was the 30 minutes after I first woke up. For the first time in decades, there wasn't a rush to get out of bed. I'd let myself fade in and out of sleep several times, savoring the fact that I could let myself fall back into that hazy sleep rather than dash into the shower to wake myself for the morning drive. I'd gotten up at 5:30 a.m. for years but found that about 7:15 a.m. was a natural time for my body to wake up. The dogs seemed to enjoy this new routine as well. We have four dogs, all of whom compete for space on the bed. Whichever one happened to be near my hand would nuzzle under my fingers when they felt me start to wake up, being content to enjoy our laziness together as a new way to start our new days.

After a relaxed cup of coffee and a bowl of cereal with my wife, I'd slip on my boots and head out into the woods for a morning walk with the dogs. When we bought our retirement cabin in the mountains, one of our criteria was to have access directly off our property into a secluded forest, which is common here given the acreage reserved as national forest land in the Appalachian Mountains. It's a criterion I'm thankful for every morning, as the one-and-a-half-mile trail through our woods has become my new retirement "commute."

The importance of planning for retirement started to demonstrate itself as the days turned into weeks and the routine of walking though those woods became a favorite part of our days. By recognizing our love of hiking and having the foresight to buy a cabin with access to trails, we've created a daily routine in retirement that will bring us joy for years to come.

As the days stretched into weeks and the weeks into months, the reality of retirement started to settle in. It's hard to explain the evolution, and I suspect everyone goes through the transition in their own unique way. For me, it was a rewarding and enjoyable experience. It was never unpleasant, but it wasn't really what I had expected, either.

With each passing day, the excitement associated with never having to work fades a bit, and the fact that this is now your life begins to settle in as a more matter-of-fact reality. The dreams about work become less frequent. Memories of student stress dreams come to mind, where for a decade after college I was still dreaming about getting lost on my way to class. The enjoyable thing about work dreams, however, is that I still smile when I wake up and realize it was just a dream. "I never have to work again," I'll think to myself. Even now, the thought still brings a smile to my face.

As the cooler fall weather began to roll in, I started getting an urge to accomplish something. I'd been enjoying my leisure for four months, and there was a natural instinct to start finding a goal to work toward. I'd always enjoyed landscaping and had been thinking of doing a major railroad tie project in the island inside our circular driveway. For the next two months, I worked an hour or two each day on my landscaping masterpiece. It was hard, physical work, and it was rewarding.

It was the first crayon drawing in my white room, and it was beautiful.

That first major project taught me that true joy in retirement is the freedom to draw whatever you'd like but also the recognition that with the freedom comes an obligation. You must draw. You must decide how you'll fill your day, and no one can do it but you. After the initial retirement thrill begins to fade, it's up to you to find a way to replace it with meaningful things.

For the next six months of retirement, I got busy drawing.

We'll talk more about how to successfully manage the transition in future chapters, but for now it's relevant to highlight the reality that your typical day in retirement will likely change over time.

≡ RETIREMENT TIP 11 ≡

Your life in retirement will change over time. Realize that the initial euphoria will fade, and enjoy the transition to a longer-term approach to retirement that works for you.

The important point is this: Recognize that your daily routine will change, and embrace the freedom to create a routine that works for you. For the first time in your life, no one else is dictating your schedule. You have complete autonomy to create the life you desire. You also have the obligation to fill your white room with those crayons you're now holding.

Some people will struggle with this transition from a life of structure to a life lived in an empty white room, and it's understandable. It's one of the biggest changes you'll go through in life, and most people don't realize how big a change it's going to be.

Now you know, and I encourage you to begin planning for it.

Buy the biggest box of crayons you can find, and begin thinking about what you want to draw on your walls. It's for your own good. Even if you're well into retirement and struggling with the transition, it's never too late to start. The walls will wait until you're ready, and you'll benefit regardless of when you decide to get serious about creating the retirement of your dreams.

If you do it right, retirement can be the most rewarding time of your life.

CREATE A NEW ROUTINE

───────○───────

It's hard to explain how big a change retirement brings to your routines. After decades of a routine that was dictated by others, your entire schedule changes on the day you retire. You no longer have to get up at 6:00 a.m. to take a shower, eat breakfast by 6:45 a.m., grab your car keys by 7:15 a.m., and be at work by 8:00 a.m. In a single day, it's all gone. That's intimidating for most and something a lot of people worry about when they think, "What will I do with all of that time?"

The good news is that you are in control of how you build your new routine, and you can build it based on whatever your preference is for how to spend your day. If you love structure, you can fill it with an organized agenda on a calendar, complete with alarms and reminders of what you need to do and when you need to do it. Prefer a more relaxed approach? No problem. Wake up and approach each day with serendipity, and enjoy the surprise of discovering where it leads.

After taking the serendipity approach for the first four months of retirement, I found I do better with a bit of structure. As my retirement evolved, I created a new routine that works for me, which is a combination of structured time in the morning and serendipity in the afternoon. Here's an example of my typical week, which should clarify the approach.

On the days that we're not traveling in our RV, I'm typically at the gym by 7:00 a.m. and I'm home by 9:00 a.m., feeling great about what I've accomplished. Whether it is attending a CrossFit class or a spin aerobics class or joining my wife for a Barre Above class, every morning of my week is in some manner or another dedicated to fitness, and I've created a structured routine to ensure I address this as a priority.

After returning from the gym, my day becomes unstructured. We still walk the dogs around the trails in our woods twice a day, but the time when this happens varies. Sometimes my wife walks them, sometimes I do, and sometimes we do it together. I'll typically carve out some time to read e-mails and manage a few things on my blog, but I don't worry if other things come up that take priority. If the weather's nice and I feel like it, I may go for an unplanned swim in a nearby lake. I may go fishing. We may go on a hike together in the mountains. We may head to town to catch an afternoon movie. We may go out for lunch. Or not.

Providing some structure early in the day gives me the freedom to do whatever I want to do with the rest of my day without feeling guilty. It took me several months of experimentation to find something that worked well for me, and I'll likely continue to modify it for years to come.

The key is to remain flexible. Don't lock yourself into a routine that you don't enjoy. Your routine is now within your control. Build it to be what you want it to be, and change it when you feel the urge to shake things up a bit. Enjoy life. You've earned it.

Relationships

Of all the changes retirement brings to life, perhaps none is larger than the impact it has on relationships. The ramifications are widespread and powerful. Strong relationships are one of the factors that bring joy to life, and your relationships are about to be rocked more severely than at any other point in your life.

I've long been fascinated with retirement and have made it a practice over the decades to intentionally spend time with coworkers who are in their final months of work. I've found that if I let them do most of the talking, soon-to-be retirees will typically share some of the things they're thinking about in their waning days of work.

Many people worry about how their relationship with their significant other will weather the transition into retirement, and this is for good reason! You've probably never spent as much time together as you're going to over the coming years. You have certain ways you do things, and you like the way your life works. Change is always difficult, and the suddenness with which retirement impacts relationships can amplify its effects. One day, your life is trending along as it has for decades. The very next day, you're together. All. The. Time.

If you haven't given considerable thought to the impact that your retirement is going to have on your relationships, you definitely should.

═ RETIREMENT TIP 12 ═

Don't retire without thinking about how
it's going to impact your relationships.
You've never spent as much time
together as you will in retirement.
Plan for it.

Some of the best advice I ever received on this topic was from a man named Jim Eberline. My wife and I had been married a few years and were expecting the birth of our daughter in the coming months. Jim was a wise man and mentored us on the value of relationships. He told us, correctly, that life would change dramatically after our child was born. "In spite of becoming parents," he said, "don't lose focus on your relationship together. Your child will become a major focal point in your life, but it's only temporary. Your marital relationship is forever. Someday your child will leave the nest, but the two of you will retire together. Always find time to foster your relationship together, and don't let your child be an excuse to let your relationship grow apart."

He'd seen too many marriages fade over the years, and it was frequently due to partners not making their relationship a priority in their lives. He dedicated his life to improving the lives of others and shared similar advice to countless young married couples over his decades as a pastor. He impacted thousands of families for good over the years, and the world lost a good man the night he died. I still miss him.

The bottom line is this: It's an unfortunate reality that many couples let their relationships drift over the years. Retirement is the time to re-prioritize your relationship. I've included some tips in the Changing Relationships feature on page 60 that include things to consider, and I encourage you to make it a priority for your retirement.

Retirement will impact almost every relationship you have in your life. After spending thousands of hours per year with people in your workplace, you'll likely never see most of those people again. We've all been through those farewell wishes when everyone promises to keep in touch, but almost no one does. Strange how that works, but it's a reality, and it will likely happen to you.

Having a good friend in the workplace has been proven to make your job more enjoyable. Unfortunately, losing that daily contact with a good friend is one of the things that can make retirement difficult. While both of you may have a desire to keep in touch, it's a difficult thing to do when one of you is still working. You can work at it—and you should—but the relationship is going to change. You'll likely grab lunch together from time to time, but you'll find that you care less about the work stuff that comes up during your chat and that your friend cares less about what you're doing in retirement. It's reality.

The social connections from work are one of the things that people miss the most after retiring and are frequently cited as a reason some people return to work in retirement. There's nothing wrong with doing that, if it's what you decide to do. We'll talk about that topic more in the upcoming chapters. For now, the point is to recognize that your relationships will change dramatically, and you should be prepared to address this.

As you get closer to The Starting Line, recognize the significance retiring will have on all of your relationships. As early as possible, work on intentionally developing "retirement relationships," which are connections with people you'll be more likely to interact with once you're no longer working.

═ RETIREMENT TIP 13 ═

Focus on developing "retirement
relationships," ideally while
you're still working.

Developing new relationships takes time and should be a focus throughout your retirement. Relationships are a key ingredient for the frosting on your retirement cake, but they won't develop by themselves. Continually seek to expand your relationships, and be intentional in striking up new friendships. An example is in order.

A year before my retirement, I happened upon a "local authors" booth at a festival in the little mountain town where we've since retired. Since I was a blogger, I mustered up the courage to walk up to the table and initiate a discussion. I looked over the books on the table from local authors and noticed several personal finance books written by someone named Ed Wolpert. Ed wasn't around, but I left my card and took one of his from the pile. Rather than leave it at that, I was intentional and followed up with an e-mail a few days later. I introduced myself and asked Ed if he'd like to meet up for lunch—my treat. That was almost three years ago, and Ed and I have become friends. I had lunch with him while I was writing this book, and he offered some great advice. Ed is a new retirement relationship, and we became friends because I decided to approach that table at the festival.

Relationships matter, and they don't grow without nourishment. Spend time developing relationships, and plant as many seeds as possible. You never know which ones will sprout into relationships, and you'll get to meet a lot of interesting people along the way. My wife and I have only been living in our mountain town for several years, but it's amazing how many people we know. We seek out opportunities to talk with people and to get to know them. We're quick to suggest a dinner out together with people who seem interesting, and we're sincerely curious about their lives. Sometimes things click, and sometimes they don't—that's fine with us, it's just the way it works.

As a result of our efforts, it's now rare for us to walk around town without seeing someone we know. When we were dreaming about our retirement, we envisioned a life in a small town where we'd stop and chat with people on Main Street. We wanted to be a part of a caring small-town community, where neighbors know each other and people say "Hi" when you pass on the sidewalk.

It's the life we drew on those white walls with our crayons, and it's become our retirement reality.

Just like relationships, our retirement reality didn't happen by chance.

CHANGING
RELATIONSHIPS

———◦———

The day after you retire, you'll start spending more time at home with loved ones. Initially, the extra time together is enjoyable. However, in time, the excessive time together can be problematic if the couple hasn't prepared for the shift in their relationship.

A story that my friend Kirk shared with me comes to mind. Kirk had traveled extensively in his career, while his wife had enjoyed her role as a stay-at-home mom focused on raising their kids. Their children had left the nest over the previous few years, and his wife had established a routine that worked well for her.

Several weeks after Kirk had retired, he had checked off most of the items on his "to-do" list and was wandering around the house as his wife loaded the dishwasher. He happened to walk up behind her as she was loading the dishwasher and questioned her about the way she was loading dishes. She became frustrated, and a "conversation" ensued. Kirk didn't mean to criticize his wife; he was just doing what he'd always done in the workplace. He saw an opportunity for improvement, and he voiced his opinion. She took it as a challenge to her ability and was frustrated by his comment. The story is a perfect example of how the increase in "together" time can cause conflict and is something most couples who have gone through the transition can relate to. Kirk and his wife have a great relationship and were able to work through the transition smoothly in time. Others aren't as fortunate.

Realize that the change resulting from retirement is as significant for a stay-at-home spouse or partner as it is for the one leaving the workplace. Take time prior to retirement to talk about your mutual expectations.

Earlier in this chapter, I promised I'd provide a few tips in this section for things to consider as you make the adjustment to more "together" time postretirement. While far from complete, the following list will give you some things to think about. I encourage you to read the list with your spouse or partner and decide on a few ground rules for your transition together.

TALK (A LOT). Make it a practice to carve out time to talk about how the transition is going. Go out for a cup of coffee together, and put your phones down. Listen twice as hard as you normally do, and repeat what you think you heard your spouse or partner say. Find a way to continue to carve out time as your retirement evolves. Sometimes, my wife and I simply sit in our living room in chairs facing each other, put down our phones, make eye contact, and talk.

ALONE VERSUS TOGETHER TIME. Discuss how much time you'd like to have together versus how much time you'd each like to have to pursue individual interests. Work together to identify things that each of you are passionate about, and be intentional in pursuing meaningful activities together and individually.

SET BOUNDARIES. Agree in advance that it's okay to raise a flag and let your spouse or partner know when you feel they're stepping on your turf. Share how the "intrusion" made you feel, and work together to learn the issues that are sensitive to the other person.

THE 80 PERCENT RULE. I remember when we were newlyweds and someone gave me a piece of advice. The advice was something to the effect that you should feel like you're sacrificing in 80 percent of situations. If both of you feel this way, the reality is you're both probably yielding about 50 percent of the time. If you don't feel you're giving in the majority of the time, you should examine whether you're being too selfish in the relationship. That guidance stuck with me, so I decided to include it for your consideration here.

DATE NIGHTS. Carve out a night every week or two to go on a date. Put them on your calendar for the next year. Use the time to focus on the positive attributes of your relationship. Like many things, you'll notice more of the things you focus on. Increase your focus on the positive, and decrease your focus on the negative.

CHAPTER

4

Hidden
Challenges

> *"Depression has been called the world's*
> *number one public health problem."*
>
> —David D. Burns,
> Stanford University School of Medicine

It's a sad reality that retirement doesn't go well for everyone. I've known people who have had successful careers yet fail miserably at retirement. I've seen good people slide into the despair. I've seen people struggle with a loss of identity and spend years of their retirement slogging unhappily without a sense of purpose. At the same time, I've seen others who are shining examples of the successful retirement we're all striving for in our lives. I suspect you've seen the same and encourage you to think about the differences between the two camps.

What's the difference between people who succeed and people who struggle in retirement? Are there lessons we can apply as we prepare for our retirement that will increase the odds of overcoming these challenges?

As I have mentioned throughout this book, I have spent a lot of time thinking about this phenomenon and have read a lot of material on what makes the difference between those who have a great retirement and those who struggle. The good news is that there are steps you can take to increase your chances of a smooth transition into retirement and achieving the successful retirement of your dreams. I found evidence that there is one single factor that is the biggest differentiator between success and struggle: preparation.

⪰ RETIREMENT TIP 15 ⪯

Take as much time as possible preparing for retirement while you're still working. It is the single biggest differentiator between success and struggle.

Earlier in this book, I mentioned the importance of the planning process as you prepare to bake your retirement cake. There was a reason I included "Invest as much time as possible into planning for your retirement" as Retirement Tip 1 and why I'm reiterating that tip again here. It turns out that the single most important thing you can do to ensure a smooth transition into retirement is to think about what you want your retirement to be like while you're still working. Recognize that your working years are coming to an end, and focus on what you want your life to become when you achieve the freedom that retirement provides. In your final working years, spend less time thinking about your work and more time thinking about your post-work life.

My hope is that this book will increase your chances of a successful retirement. As part of that quest, it's important that we discuss potential challenges you may face. Not everyone will experience these challenges, and among those who do there will be some variability in the intensity and appearance of the symptoms. If you find yourself struggling, this chapter will help get you back on track.

Common Challenges: Identified

The following are some of the common challenges people face as they make the transition from decades of work to their new life of a self-directed retirement. The list is not intended to be comprehensive, but it provides a summary of the challenges that you should be thinking about as you make your way down the road of retirement.

Be self-aware as you begin your journey, and seek out opportunities to talk to other people in your life as you adjust to your new reality. If you have a spouse or partner, find time to have meaningful discussions together. It is also suggested that you be cognizant that "gray divorce" is also a challenge that some people face as they find themselves spending more time together. Gray divorce refers to the trend of increasing divorce rates among people over the age of 50, which has doubled over the past 20 years while the overall divorce rate has declined. Open up your chains of communication now, even if it's a change from the relationship you've had in the past. You're both going through this together, so foster a relationship in which you can help each other make the adjustments required to minimize the negative impacts of your transition.

DEPRESSION

*"Retirement from work has depressed
many a man and hastened his death."*
—Ezra Taft Benson

When I was two years away from retirement, I wrote an article titled "Will Retirement Be Depressing?" It was a culmination of the research I had been conducting at the time on those who struggled with retirement. I read a study by the Institute of Economic Affairs that found that a person's probability of suffering from clinical depression goes up by 40 percent after retiring. Other studies have confirmed the reality that depression is more likely in retirement than during a person's working years.

During my research, I found that it's not uncommon to experience a bit of depression as you move from the structure that your work life provided to the unstructured life of retirement. If you find yourself struggling with depression, experiment with various methods to add some structure into your life. Commit to a few things that require appointments on your calendar, like the fitness classes I attend each morning. Sign up for some e-mails from blogs and newsletters so your inbox will have a regular flow of healthy food for your brain. Get engaged with a charity or join a group that holds regular meetings in your area. Building some structure can be the first step in overcoming depression in your early days of retirement.

My wife experienced a bout of mild depression shortly after our retirement. We'll explore her situation in more detail in chapter 5, but suffice it to say that her experience matches what the studies conclude. After 25 years of providing care for others, she suddenly found herself without a purpose in retirement, which is often the primary reason people experience depression. I won't provide the solution to her problem here, but I encourage you to read her story in chapter 5.

Speaking of chapter 5, there's a reason it's in this book. In my opinion it's the most important chapter, and I wouldn't write a book about the keys to a successful retirement without it. Losing a sense of purpose in life often leads people to a bad place, and finding a new purpose is often the most effective road to recovery. If you find yourself struggling with depression as you make the transition into retirement, pay special attention to chapter 5, and focus on the importance of finding a new sense of purpose in your life.

In addition to working on developing a purpose for your retirement, there are some simple steps you can take that may be less overwhelming than attempting to find your purpose in life. Research has found that getting direct sunlight (outside, not through a window) can be helpful when dealing with depression. In addition to establishing some routines, research suggests finding ways to be social and having meaningful conversations with friends. I encourage you to combine all three suggestions and create a weekly schedule with a daily walk outside and at least one meal a week with friends. Focus on the positive, and don't be afraid (or too proud) to seek help if you need it. Resources are provided at the end of this book should you wish to seek professional help.

BOREDOM

"I don't think I'll ever retire.
I don't know what I'd do all day."
—Anonymous

Have you ever had anyone say that to you? I suspect you have, given how common this sentiment is among people of retirement age. Many people love their work and worry that they'd be bored without the daily activity their job provides. Unfortunately, even if you love your work, there will likely come a day when you'll have to retire, whether by choice or by circumstances outside your control.

Even for those who are excited about the prospects of a life without the obligation of work, you've likely asked yourself the question "Will I get bored?" I don't know too many people who were more excited about retirement than I was, and yet I found myself asking the same question.

It's a normal worry.

Life in retirement does not have to mean a life of boredom sitting in your recliner watching TV all day, every day. However, it's up to you to decide how you want to live your life of freedom. Without any effort to plan ahead and develop outside interests, it's certainly possible that yours will be a life of boredom.

It happens.

If it happens to you, you'll have no one to blame but yourself. Perhaps that's a tough message, but it's true. Unlike the workplace, where you have a boss who tells you what to do, retirement is an entirely different animal.

You are the boss.

You set the rules. You set the schedule. You set the agenda. Isn't that exactly the freedom that excites you about retirement? It's also the reason you probably worry about being bored. You've never had this level of freedom before, and you're not sure how you're going to handle it. Don't worry—there are thousands who have walked this journey before you, and there are lessons you can learn if you study the things that have worked for others.

To minimize the risk of boredom in retirement, start working now on finding new activities to pursue during your retirement. However small these interests are, start writing down ideas for things you'd like to try. Build a bucket list of things you'd like to accomplish, and stretch yourself to go beyond the obvious "travel" ideas. Build a list for personal development. Throw in a few ideas to stretch your artistic side. Think about physical activities that have interested you but you've never had time to pursue. Look online for clubs in your area, and sign up now for their e-mail list. Check out volunteer opportunities, and test out a few during an upcoming weekend. Focus on creating as large a list as possible, and look it over if you ever get bored in retirement.

In our case, the best thing we did was to create a "retirement activity jar" a year before my retirement date. My wife and I each filled out slips of paper with activities we wanted to do in retirement. We each tried to come up with one new idea every week, and we never shared our ideas with each other. By the time I retired 52 weeks later, we had two years' worth of weekly activities stuffed in our jar, half of which were a complete surprise for each of us. It's been fun pulling out a slip of paper every week and trying a new activity, and it's kept us from becoming bored.

Will you get bored in retirement?

Only you can answer that question.

After all, you're the boss.

LOSS OF IDENTITY

> "If you are what you do,
> who are you when you don't?"
> —Richard J. Leider and Alan M. Webber (from *Life Reimagined: Discovering Your New Life Possibilities*)

Most people feel a loss of identity when they leave the workplace. It's understandable, given that we've long answered the common question of "What do you do?" with a response focused on our work. Work has defined us for decades, and it's normal to feel a loss of identity when we can no longer claim to be an accountant, a salesperson, a manager, or whatever it was that we did for a living.

This is common, and your discomfort in answering this question will improve as you redefine yourself in retirement. Be patient and take some time to think about what you want to be known for in your retirement years. Are you most proud of being a grandparent, or would you prefer to be known for creating something? Is there a particular project that you're focused on that you'd like people to know about? You are free from being defined by a job you were once paid to do. It's an exciting reality that your new identity is entirely up to you to define. It can be intimidating, but it's an exercise worth pursuing in retirement. Not only will it help with a loss of identity, but it will help shape what it is that you want to become. Done correctly, defining yourself can lead to a life of purpose in retirement.

Since I've retired, I've responded to the "What do you do?" question with a combination of things that I've decided to be defined by. My typical response is along the lines of "I chose to retire early, and I'm enjoying doing whatever I choose to do. I've discovered that I love writing and enjoy working on my retirement blog. My wife and I also enjoy traveling in our RV and recently returned from a nice trip visiting our daughter in the Pacific Northwest." People tend to follow up with questions about whatever part of my response piqued their interest. It's all good to me, since each of these are a part of what I've become.

Don't focus on the identity you lost when you left the workplace. Focus on what you're becoming. Come up with an enticing "elevator speech" on what you're doing in retirement, and challenge yourself to engage people in deeper conversation when they ask, "What do you do?"

I remember the first time I went out in a sea kayak and forgot to put the rudder down. It was difficult to keep the boat going in a straight line until someone pointed out that my rudder was sticking up in the air. I flipped the rudder down, and my kayak's performance improved immediately.

Just like in a kayak, life is more enjoyable when you have a rudder helping you hold your course.

Discover your rudder.

Define your direction.

GRIEF

"Grief is in two parts. The first is loss.
The second is the remaking of life."
—Anne Roiphe

I've been through numerous "downsizings" during my 33-year career, and it seems the struggle with grief often hits those who were unexpectedly forced into retirement. I mentioned in chapter 1 that it's common for people to be forced into retirement earlier than planned. In an article I wrote titled "Will You Be Forced to Retire Early?," I found some research from Voya Financial that cited a full 60 percent of people retire earlier than they had planned. It's a startling statistic and reflects the reality that life often throws unexpected curves in our paths. Between health issues, caring for aging parents, taking care of a sick spouse or partner, and downsizings, it's more likely than not that you'll retire sooner than you think.

For people who have been forced into retirement, it's common to go through a grieving process. We're proud of what we do, and it's natural to feel a loss when we give up our jobs unexpectedly. Unlike those who are able to plan far in advance for their retirement date, people who leave suddenly have not been able to prepare for the significant shift that retirement represents. They find themselves unexpectedly removed from their friends at work and the predictability of their working routine, and the suddenness of an unplanned retirement often results in feelings of grief and depression.

If you find yourself forced into retirement, don't be surprised if you suffer some of the challenges outlined in this chapter. Losing a job is one of the most stressful things you can go through in life, and it's normal to feel what you're feeling. Your sense of security has been rocked, and it's going to take some time to pick yourself back up. Allow time for the transition to happen, and think of your job loss as a temporary setback. You may not have chosen to be in this situation, but you can choose your path forward.

Resist the urge to withdraw from social interaction, which is common following the embarrassment of losing your job. Interaction with others is an important part of overcoming the grief you're experiencing, so make it a priority to find others you can talk to as you work through your situation. Find a friend you can exercise with, even if it's an easy walk around your neighborhood. Fresh air, exercise, and social interaction will all be helpful as you deal with your grief.

If you really aren't ready to retire, there's nothing wrong with pursuing another job. Unfortunately, jobs are harder to land as we age, and it's important to recognize that it may take some time. Rather than focusing on a single path forward, pursue multiple paths. Consider the possibility that you'll never land the type of job you've been forced to leave, and be honest with yourself about your options. Consider pursuing some part-time work while you think through what's truly important for you and how you want to spend the rest of your life. While you're looking for work, get engaged in charity work to provide some social engagement and goodwill in your life. Focus on doing something that brings you purpose, and consider your situation as an opportunity to change your life for the better.

Common Challenges: Methods of Attack

Every day, 10,000 Baby Boomers turn 65, and many of them will struggle with their transition to retirement. As you read through these methods of attack, choose several that resonate with you and give them a try.

First, if you're not yet retired, spend as much time as possible prior to your retirement thinking about what you want your life to be in retirement. Again, this is the biggest difference between those who have a great retirement and those who struggle. There is a strong correlation between the amount of effort you put into planning for your retirement and the resulting success when you ultimately transition. Begin building a life outside work as early as possible, and ramp up these external interests as you get closer to your retirement date. Think about developing alternative means of fulfilling the socialization and self-worth you currently receive from the workplace, and be intentional in growing these options in your final years of work.

If you've already retired, try not to obsess about the fact that you're finding the transition different than you expected. As mentioned in chapter 3, there's no way to know what this transition is going to be like until you go through it yourself. In much the same way as you adjust your stride when you first step off a moving sidewalk, there will be some major adjustments in your life as you leave the workplace. You're certainly not alone, and you can find assurance in the fact that many others have struggled before you and found their path to a great retirement. There are professionals who are available to help you apply the same lessons others have used, so don't hesitate to lean on them to help you sort things out. This is a new reality, and it's common for the adjustment to take some time.

Relax and give yourself a moment to settle into your new life. You have decades of wonderful living ahead of you, so take your time in feeling your way through the transition. The following are some tips to help smooth your transition.

STAY ACTIVE

Find ways to keep both your mind and your body active. The words of Andrew Weil, MD, are relevant: "Human bodies are designed for regular physical activity. The sedentary nature of much of modern life probably plays a significant role in the epidemic incidence of depression today. Many studies show that depressed patients who stick to a regimen of aerobic exercise improve as much as those treated with medication." Find a friend who will meet you for a walk each day. Join a local gym or a hiking club. Get outside and absorb some sunlight—you've earned that right. Don't fall into the trap of watching too much TV, which will likely do more harm than good. You feel better when you're fit, and it will benefit you in many ways as you age. If you've never gotten serious about taking care of yourself, now is the time to start.

STRENGTHEN SOCIAL RELATIONSHIPS

Intentionally seek out others, and don't suffer alone. Schedule time to visit your kids, or offer to watch your grandchildren. Find a group of friends and go to breakfast with them once a week and talk about what you're dealing with in your transition. Reread chapter 3 and consider ways to strengthen your relationship with your spouse or partner. If you struggle talking about what you're going through, schedule an appointment with your doctor or consider online counseling (see Finding Your Passion Resources on page 125).

FIND A NEW SENSE OF PURPOSE

We'll dig deeper into this topic in the next chapter, but it's important to find something to replace the meaning once provided by your work. Focus more on others and less on yourself. Finding ways to help other people brings a sense of fulfillment that will help in your transition. Find a way to be generous with your time in a local charity or in support of a cause you feel deeply about.

FOCUS ON YOUR SPIRITUALITY

Now that your time is free from the constraints previously imposed by work, take time to be introspective and think about things of higher importance. Try spending some time each day in prayer, meditation, or reflection. Focusing on things of eternal consequence will help put your current struggles into perspective. We would all be wise to heed these words from T. Boone Pickens, written shortly before his death: "Have faith, both in spiritual matters and in humanity, and in yourself. That faith will see you through the dark times we all navigate."

FULFILL YOUR DREAMS

Think about something you've always wanted to do, and make a plan to do it. We never know how long our health will last, so do something "big" while you have the opportunity. Consider taking that trip you've always dreamed of, or learn to play that instrument you've always wanted to play. Use your newfound freedom to do something for you and enjoy the excitement of doing something you've always wanted to do.

DEVELOP A SCHEDULE

The loss of structure that your job provided is often a cause of struggle in the post-work transition. Experiment with different methods of building structure into your day. As I mentioned in chapter 3, I've found I feel better if I add some structured exercise early in my day while leaving the afternoon open for unstructured activities. Perhaps you'd prefer to commit a few days a week to a regular activity, such as dedicated charity work. Don't get stuck in a rut: Be willing to change things up until you find something that works for you.

⟹RETIREMENT TIP 16⟸

If you're struggling with your transition to retirement, don't hesitate to reach out for help. There are people who dedicate their lives to helping people. Let them help you.

There can be nothing as frustrating as other people telling you, "Relax, everything is going to be fine." Sometimes the reality is that you're getting worse instead of better and you find yourself unable to work through the issues on your own. Without taking action, your symptoms could become more severe and reach the point of true crisis.

Some symptoms of more serious problems include:

→ Continually feeling sad, depressed, or empty

→ Difficulty getting out of bed in the morning or perpetual tiredness

- ➤ Finding that things you used to enjoy aren't of interest anymore

- ➤ Having difficulty sleeping

- ➤ Increasing irritability, restlessness, or anxiety

- ➤ Loss of appetite or serious weight gain

- ➤ Difficulty thinking or making decisions

- ➤ Loss of self-esteem

- ➤ Feeling worthless, helpless, guilty, or hopeless

- ➤ Thinking about death or suicide

If you're finding yourself falling deeper into depression or other personal struggles, don't hesitate to reach out for help. Read the following feature for some additional thoughts on the value of reaching out for help, and use the Finding Your Passion Resources section (see page 125) to contact people who dedicate their lives to helping people through difficult times. Whatever you do, please don't suffer in silence. If you need help, seek it.

REACHING OUT

Joe Rubbo was my biology teacher in high school, and he was one of the best teachers I ever had. I'll always remember an important lesson he taught me more than 40 years ago. We had just taken a field trip to a mental health facility and had witnessed firsthand the devastating effect that mental-health challenges can have on a person's life. We were allowed to walk through one of the wards in the facility and had conversations with several of the patients. I recall in particular one middle-aged woman who was pencil-thin and ranted endlessly in a confused stream of anxiety. I've wondered what happened to that woman ever since the day of my visit.

The visit was devastating and depressing. It also led to one of the most powerful lessons I've learned in life.

Back in our classroom the next day, Mr. Rubbo made a comment that resonates with me to this day. "If you learned nothing else from the field trip, remember this," he said. "Everyone goes through struggles in their life. It's an unavoidable part of the process. What's important is that you recognize the fact that struggles are normal and there's nothing wrong with you if you're having problems. What's more important is that you never keep your problems to yourself. If you're having serious problems, don't hesitate to reach out for help. There are people who have committed their lives to helping others deal with the problems they face. Remember what you saw yesterday, and never hesitate to reach out for help."

It's important that we talk about the reality of retirement challenges. If you find yourself struggling through your transition into retirement, please listen to the life lesson I learned so many years ago from Mr. Rubbo.

If you're having issues dealing with one of the biggest transitions you'll make in life, don't be too proud to reach out. Never hesitate to ask for help. Mr. Rubbo died of cancer in his early 30s. I regret that he's not alive to read these words, to know that he made an impression that lasted my entire life. Don't do it for me. Don't do it for Mr. Rubbo. Do it for you. If these words are resonating with you, we both have Mr. Rubbo to thank. If there's any way you can read these words, Mr. Rubbo, I offer a heartfelt "thank you" for one of the most important lessons I've ever learned in life.

I've compiled a list of resources (see page 125) if you need to seek some help. Send an e-mail. Make a phone call. Do it now. Please.

21st-Century Challenges

Retirement in the 21st century is unlike the retirement our parents and grandparents faced. Gone are the days of generous pensions and employer-sponsored health care for retirees. While we have unique challenges, it's also fair to recognize that today's technology provides opportunities that previous generations could have never imagined. Free online education? Driverless cars? Video chats?

The reality is there are pros and cons for those who are retiring in today's world, just as there were for retirees in the past. Our challenges may seem more significant than those of our predecessors, but we're also fortunate to have a world in which technological advancements will lead to material improvements in our lives. With that said, let's look at a few of the hidden challenges we face as retirees in the 21st century.

HEALTH CARE

For those living in the United States, health insurance is likely one of the biggest challenges you're facing as you consider retirement, especially if you're retiring before age 65. Concerns about private health insurance are often cited as the primary reason people decide to continue working until they become eligible for Medicare at age 65. Personally, I find it depressing to think that people are working solely for the sake of health insurance and would encourage you to consider your alternatives. I'm also a realist and recognize that many people have no other viable option. It's a serious problem, one that will likely linger for years.

In our case, I retired at age 55 in spite of the need to buy private health insurance for 10 years. When I was building our retirement spending forecast, I used a conservative estimated health insurance cost of $2,500/month with a

5 percent inflation adjustment every year. I wanted to be conservative in our estimate, given the serious risks in this area of retirement planning. Once we had accumulated 30x our estimated spending requirement level, which included the high insurance estimate, we made the decision to retire in spite of the health insurance risks. If you're considering private insurance, make sure you've investigated the details of the Affordable Care Act, and determine if you may be eligible for income-based subsidies. If eligible, these subsidies can be a significant help in finding affordable health insurance in the marketplace.

For those without the means to pay for private insurance, it's worth mentioning the option of health care sharing ministries (HCSMs), which are typically Christian groups in which members share the health care costs incurred by other members. HCSMs have become more popular as the price of private insurance has increased in recent years, but it's important to realize that they're not the same as traditional insurance. In fact, as you review HCSM options, you'll find they're very careful to avoid insurance-type wording. My biggest concern regarding HCSMs is the fact that they are under no obligation to pay your medical claims and can deny a claim without repercussion. That said, I have friends who are content with their HCSM coverage and are pleased with this lower-cost solution.

In the Retirement Resources (see page 115), you'll find relevant online resources for retiree health care coverage, including some links to HCSMs.

TECHNOLOGY

Technology is ever-evolving, and many people find themselves out of touch with the latest advancements soon after they leave the workplace. We all know older people who are intimidated by computers, and we run the risk of becoming out-of-date ourselves.

Challenge yourself to stay up-to-date as technology changes and seek out advancements that could improve your life in retirement. Stay informed by intentionally watching the technology headlines instead of avoiding the topic. Seek out free educational opportunities, some of which I've included on page 133. Did you know, for example, that you can take free courses at your local Apple store? Apple offers free interactive, hands-on classes for a variety of skill levels. If you have an interest in a certain topic, do a search on YouTube and you'll be on your way to learning a new skill. Coursera offers free online classes, many from esteemed universities. Rather than be intimidated by technology, view it as an opportunity and challenge yourself to continue to grow through your retirement years.

One of the items on my retirement bucket list was to teach myself how to edit videos. I knew absolutely nothing about video editing but wanted a personal challenge and a skill I could utilize in retirement. I purchased some video editing software and searched YouTube to find a few videos that showed me how to get started. I'm proud to say that I now have a YouTube channel with several videos from our cross-country RV trip. I've also created a YouTube channel for my wife's nonprofit (Freedom For Fido), and I have uploaded several videos of dog fence projects we've built for low-income families in our area.

RETIREMENT TIP 17

Never stop learning. View technology as
a means to personal growth, and seek
out opportunities to continually learn in
your retirement years.

Only you can determine how you'll view technological changes throughout your retirement. You can choose to ignore them and become out-of-date, or you can seek out opportunities to enhance your retirement by accessing all that technology has to offer. I've chosen the latter and encourage you to do the same. Pick one of the free educational opportunities included on page 133, and sign up for a class. Never stop learning.

FINANCIAL CLIMATE

Our culture is facing a level of divisiveness not seen since the Civil War. While this is concerning on a societal level, it's also a 21st-century challenge that we should consider as we plan for our retirements. As the political winds continue to blow, the reality is that our retirements may be seriously impacted by cultural factors. Governments throughout the world have committed to massive obligations through programs designed to assist retirees, and we're naive if we think those programs do not face some risk as a result of increasing cultural discontent.

Programs such as Medicare and Social Security, for example, could fall under increased "means testing" legislation, where those who have more could be required to subsidize those who have less. If you're fortunate to have saved a lot of eggs for your retirement cake, recognize that you may be impacted. These two funds consumed 45 percent of federal program expenditures in 2018, and they're likely to face increasing scrutiny as the growing population of Baby Boomer retirees places further burdens on the programs.

In 2020, the total costs of Social Security are projected to exceed its total income for the first time since 1982. After 2035, current projections are that only 75 percent of Social Security expenses will be covered by scheduled tax income. It's possible that future benefits will be reduced or workers of the future will be burdened with higher costs to support the program. In our planning, we included only 75 percent of our "promised" Social Security benefits in our retirement cash flow to ensure that we were building in a bit of a buffer in the event that future benefits are impacted by changing legislation or economic factors. I encourage you to factor a buffer into your planning as well.

Growing concerns about income inequality could lead to legislation that reduces the benefits of federal programs for people who have been responsible in saving for retirement. Millions of people have undersaved for retirement, and political pressure could build to protect those who are deemed less fortunate. Income tax rates could certainly rise as governments seek additional income to offset the growing costs of funding various programs designed to act as a safety net or to provide income to retirees. As your before-tax money begins to be impacted by the required minimum distribution requirements outlined in chapter 2, it's possible you'll be taxed at higher marginal tax rates than you're paying today.

Keep abreast of these and other factors in today's financial and political climate. I'd encourage you to read the annual statement from the trustees of the programs mentioned and keep informed on developments that may impact your retirement.

WHAT IF YOU BECOME INCAPACITATED?

———◦———

None of us are going to live on this earth forever. At some point, you will die. Between now and then, there's a good chance that you'll face serious health challenges that may incapacitate you. Perhaps you'll face a future stricken with Alzheimer's, in which you'll lose your ability to manage anything in your life. Morbid thought, but it's best to be transparent about the realities of our later retirement years and address what options are available while we still can.

As we think about the hidden challenges of our retirements, I'd be irresponsible if I didn't include a section on what you should do to plan for the potential of becoming incapacitated. Fortunately, there are means to address these situations, and I encourage you to take the steps necessary to protect yourself and your family against the possibility that you'll be impacted.

Following are the three legal documents you should put in place now, if you haven't already:

WILL. Everyone should have a will, which is essentially a document that says who gets what when you die. If you don't create a will, the state will get involved upon your death and distribute the assets based on its own laws. You should also select an estate administrator, who will have the responsibility of settling your estate. If it's been more than five years since you've updated your will, put a reminder on your calendar to update yours in the coming weeks.

LIVING WILL. This document, often called a health care directive, outlines the treatments you would and would not want to be used to keep you alive as well as your preferences for other medical decisions (e.g., organ donation). Without a living will, doctors will do everything in their power to keep you alive, including the use of life support, which may be against your wishes.

POWER OF ATTORNEY. The person you designate in your power of attorney (POA) has legal authority to make decisions on your behalf when you are no longer capable of making sound decisions. A medical POA authorizes a person to make medical decisions on your behalf, while a financial POA authorizes someone to handle your finances. You should have both in place as a durable POA, which ensures they will be valid after you become incapacitated.

You should also check all of your financial accounts to ensure that your beneficiaries (those people who you've identified to receive your assets upon your death) are updated and match the desires outlined in your will. While you're at it, make sure you've placed your accounts in the appropriate structure to have them pass directly to the beneficiary upon your death rather than needing to be involved in the probate process. We have our accounts set up as joint trusts with rights of survivorship (JTWROS), a standard designation. Finally, make sure you've identified an appropriate advocate who can act on your behalf, and have a serious discussion with them about your wishes before you identify them in your legal documents.

═ RETIREMENT TIP 18 ═

Take the time to put the
appropriate legal safeguards in
place, and find a time to talk with
your family about your wishes.

A few years ago, when we were home for Christmas, my dad scheduled a meeting with his attorney to give us an overview of the legal documents he had prepared. It was encouraging to know my dad had put everything in place to address various situations that could arise, and it was a good example of a conversation that everyone should have with their family. I'm proud of my dad for the way he handled it, and it felt good to be able to tell him that after our meeting. If you've not done so, schedule a date to communicate your wishes to your family and ensure they have copies of the relevant documents "just in case."

CHAPTER

5

Embracing Passion to Create Your Ideal Retirement

> *"The two most important days in your life are the day you are born . . . and the day you find out why."*
>
> —Author Unknown

I first noticed his WWII Veteran hat as I boarded a plane in Paris during the last international business trip of my career. When the 90-year-old man sat down just six rows ahead of me, I knew I had to find a way to talk to him during the flight home. Mid-ocean, I approached, knelt down beside him in the aisle, thanked him for his service, and asked if he'd mind if I asked him a quick question. "Sure," he said, smiling. "I'm not doing anything else for the next few hours." That quick question turned into an amazing 45-minute conversation that I will carry with me for the rest of my life.

Why Passion and Purpose Are Essential in Creating a Successful Retirement

Why was I asking an older stranger a question over the middle of the ocean? He was the latest victim in my One Retirement Question project, an initiative I launched on my blog a few months before my retirement. It started serendipitously as I was talking with an older couple who were enjoying a wonderful retirement. A thought struck as we talked, and I decided to run with it. After checking with them that it would be okay, I pulled out my phone, hit record, and then asked them a question: *"If you could give ONE piece of advice to someone who is 30 days away from retirement, what would it be?"*

The answers I received to that question taught me that *finding a passion or purpose is the most important thing you can do for a successful retirement.* Representing more than 100 years of successful retirement living, the retirees I interviewed all touched on the importance of the same piece of advice: They all had to do with purpose. None of the interviewees heard the response from the others, yet they all answered with similar advice. I found the consistency amazing, and it convinced me that finding a passion is the true key to a successful retirement.

Following are a few of the responses:

- → "Try to accomplish one goal every day. Have a purpose."—Mrs. Smith, age 76

- → "Have long-term goals and short-term goals every day that keep you going physically and mentally. Be a doer."—Dad, age 84

- → "Plan to stay active, physically and mentally, at all times."—Don Matthews, age 90

➜ "Be passionate about something and develop that passion as much as you possibly can."—Uncle Carl, age 79

➜ "Jump in and enjoy this new chapter in your life. Stay busy, don't stop."—Curtis, age 82

➜ "Stay busy. Stay happy."—P.R., age 94

Finding something meaningful to accomplish in retirement is the true "frosting on the cake," and I consider this chapter the most important of this book. I always seek opportunities to learn from others who have walked the path before me, and I learned a lot from the wise elders interviewed during my One Retirement Question project. In subsequent research, the theme of pursuing meaningful activities consistently shows up as one of the top keys to a successful retirement.

For years, we've not had the freedom to do the things that we care deeply about. The demands of the workplace and the golden handcuffs associated with the need for that paycheck kept us dutifully distracted by the requirements of our jobs. We were building up our nest egg, just waiting for that point in our lives where we'd have the freedom to do what we wanted to do. Just waiting to get through that miserable commute. Just waiting to get through another useless meeting. Just waiting . . .

The waiting is now over.

Retirement is a new reality, and it's the time we've been waiting for. Gone are all of those constraints that accompany the need to earn money. Eliminating the need to earn a paycheck is bigger than it appears on the surface. Without the need to work for pay, we're free to pursue the things in our lives that really matter. The things that bring real fulfillment. The things that provide us with self-worth. The things that bring meaning. THIS is what a successful retirement is all about.

For the first time since childhood, we no longer require the financial motives to be a consideration behind our actions. Free from the need to earn a paycheck, the motives that drive your actions in retirement are different from those that have driven you for decades. Figuring out what you're going to do and why you're going to do it is what your focus in retirement must be. Do it right, and the next few decades will be the best of your life.

What's required to "do it right"? What's the one key ingredient that will increase the odds of a successful and meaningful retirement? If you believe the respondents to that One Question, it's pretty simple. Now that you have a bit more context, I'd encourage you to flip back and reread those responses. Enlightening, right?

Passion represents having our actions driven by things that matter more than money. Finding a passion represents finding things you deeply enjoy and then dedicating your energy in that direction and watching where it leads. This is real living. This is the life that you've been waiting for. Passion matters. Finding your passion has even been shown to increase longevity and reduce the risk of cognitive decline.

═ RETIREMENT TIP 19 ═

Rather than thinking about seeking your passion, ask yourself, "What can I do with my time that's important?" Committing your energy to something that matters to you is the true frosting on your retirement cake.

During our working years we were forced to do things that we didn't care all that much about. Now that we've achieved financial independence, we have a limited opportunity to pursue the things that bring deeper meaning to our lives. Things that are driven by motives that matter more than money. Things in which we enjoy the rewards of giving back and putting others ahead of ourselves.

Now is the time to move from success to significance.

We're walking through that white room and getting closer to the exit door to eternity with every passing day. What really matters to you? What are you going to draw on those walls? It's the most important question you can ask yourself in retirement. Don't look back on how you answer that question and end up with regrets.

Speaking of regrets, one of the more powerful things I've read was an article from Bronnie Ware, a palliative care nurse who wrote about her experiences with dying patients. She said people gain "phenomenal clarity of vision" at the end of their lives, and common themes surfaced again and again from people in their final days.

The top five regrets are worth reflecting on as we enter our golden years. As you think about what you're going to do with the once-in-a-lifetime opportunity presented by your retirement, consider what others have regretted not doing and seek to take action now to avoid these regrets on your deathbed:

1. *I wish I'd had the courage to live a life true to myself, not the life others expected of me.*

2. *I wish I hadn't worked so hard.*

3. *I wish I had the courage to express my feelings.*

4. *I wish I had stayed in touch with my friends.*

5. *I wish that I had let myself be happier.*

Retirement is the time to live a life that matters to you. It's up to you to make it happen.

How to Progress

Do you remember when you were a child and the final day of school was approaching? Chances are you didn't do much planning for your summer break. You were free, so what was there to worry about? Summer was finally here, and you were looking forward to doing whatever you wanted to do over the next few months. Freedom!

If you were like me, you were bored by the middle of July.

Retirement is a summer vacation that extends for years, and we can't run the risk of destroying our final summer vacation with boredom that leads to regret. Let's learn from our childhood and do it differently this time. This time it is for real. This time it really matters.

Let's talk about some practical steps you may want to consider. They've worked well for me, and I hope they give you some fodder as you sort out how you're going to spend your retirement years.

FOCUS ON PLANNING

Unlike our childhood summers, take some time before school is out to think about what you're going to do with your summer vacation. You'll notice that this is the third time I've mentioned the importance of planning. That's intentional— it's the single biggest differentiator on which direction your retirement will go in.

From a practical standpoint, consider taking a "test retirement" about a year before your retirement begins. In my case, I did it during a Thanksgiving holiday break. I extended the break by taking an extra week off and pretended I was retired. I fought the urge to check my e-mail, and my wife and I spent the time thinking about what we wanted our retirement to be like. It was the first time I started to think seriously about purpose. Take some time during your mini-retirement experiment and think about the following questions:

→ What will your life look like when work is no longer mandatory?

→ How will you spend your time?

→ What will give you purpose?

TAKE TIME TO ESTABLISH GUIDELINES FOR HOW YOU WANT TO LIVE YOUR LIFE IN RETIREMENT

Three months before I retired, I made a list of guidelines for how I wanted to live my life during my retirement years, and I posted the list on the wall in my office. Here's what I came up with:

→ Have an attitude of gratitude

→ Give with a generous heart

→ Pursue passions

→ Keep the balance

→ Make no obligations

→ Try new things

→ Take care of your body

→ Stay flexible to change

→ Cherish friends and family

→ Have fun

→ Keep eternity in mind

Looking back at my list with the perspective of time, I'm happy with what I chose to prioritize as my guidelines in retirement. I believe that making a conscious decision to maintain a positive attitude is one of the best things you can do as you approach retirement. I'm also pleased that I recognized the importance of pursuing passions before I really understood what it meant. I encourage you to come up with a list that outlines your priorities and make a habit of reviewing it as your retirement evolves.

BEGIN TO EXPERIMENT WITH AS MANY NEW ACTIVITIES AS POSSIBLE

Finding a passion is a nebulous affair and one that is best found via serendipity. Throw as many things as possible against the wall, and see what sticks. For me, one of the things that stuck and became a passion was writing. If you'd have asked me a few years ago, I'd have never listed writing as an area that would provide meaning in my retirement years. And yet, now that I'm living life as a retiree, it's an activity that gives me a reason for being. It's hard to describe the satisfaction that comes from the regular flow of feedback from my readers about the positive impact I'm making in their lives. I'm making a difference. I'm giving back. I've found something that keeps me mentally stimulated. I'm having a ball.

≡ RETIREMENT TIP 20 ≡

Throw as many things as possible
against the wall, and see what sticks.

For me, it was writing. For my childhood friend, David, it was rediscovering his childhood love of photography. For you, it will likely be something else. Regardless, the simple process I followed can be applied by anyone.

Three years before I retired, my wife went away on a trip with a friend for a weekend. On Friday afternoon, I wrote up a list of things I wanted to accomplish while she was gone. On that list were three simple words that led to places I'd have never dreamed: "Start a blog." It all starts with taking a first step. Think about things that interest you, and determine your first step. Throw it against the wall.

Recognize that most of the things will slide to the floor. That's all part of the process, so learn to enjoy it. I've thrown a lot of things up there, but only a few have become things that bring real meaning. Think broadly, and throw anything up there that comes to mind.

I once knew a guy who committed suicide, and it's a memory that will haunt me my entire life. I realize that's a horrible sentence to throw into this discussion, but there's a lesson I learned from the terrible situation that is applicable here. I was 23 years old and taking an eight-week Dale Carnegie course as a new sales trainee. On week six of the class, we noticed that our classmate Bob was missing and asked where he was. The instructor said, "Bob committed suicide last night. Let me say this, if I may. I like to think of life as a wheel and how all the aspects of your life can be represented by spokes. There's faith, family, money, work, relationships, etc. All of the elements in our lives are the spokes on our wheel. Turns out that Bob had a bunch of uneven spokes and his wheel didn't roll very well." Powerful stuff that has impacted me ever since.

The words that Charles Hobbs wrote in *Time Power* are relevant. He wrote that a balanced life had six components:

1. *Spiritual: What kind of person do you want to be? What are your views on eternity?*

2. *Social: What are your key relationships, and what do you want to accomplish in them?*

3. *Professional: What do you want to accomplish in your job? What do you want to be doing?*

4. *Physical: Are you properly addressing your health, activity, and diet?*

5. *Intellectual / Cultural: How do you want to feed your mind, and with what?*

6. *Financial: How will you use the money you have to achieve your other goals?*

As you think of things to try, pursue areas that represent all of the spokes in your wheel of life, and focus on keeping your wheel well balanced. Do an assessment of your values and goals. Write a list of your retirement priorities, such as charity, faith, family, and interests. Think about the things you wanted to do when you were a child. Think about people who influenced you. Pick a few that are most important to you, and figure out what you need to do to get started on a few items in those areas. Then simply take that first step and see where it leads.

⟩ RETIREMENT TIP 21 ⟨

Seek to develop interests for all the spokes in your life. A wheel rolls best when the spokes are the same length.

As you develop new passions, set personal goals in each of the areas. Monitoring your progress can provide the motivation and structure you once received from work. If you decide to start walking, for example, challenge yourself with a weekly mileage goal. Have some fun, and continually seek out new ways to fulfill the areas in your life that motivate you. Keep an open mind, and try anything that challenges you, that keeps you engaged, that allows you to give back. Recognize what you miss from work, and build new areas into your life that meet these needs.

If you find you're longing for the social interaction, personal challenge, or sense of purpose that work once provided, it's fine to consider going back to work, perhaps on a part-time basis. In my post "UnRetirement: The Facts," I cite the reality that 25 percent of people "un-retire," and most do so for nonfinancial reasons. In the book *Victory Lap Retirement*, Mike Drak, Rob Morrison, and Jonathan Chevreau use the analogy of someone who takes a victory lap after they've won the race. I picture a NASCAR race, where the winner drives slowly around the track waving a flag. The victory lap is run more slowly and for a different purpose than the race itself, and it brings its own unique reward. See page 127 for this and other books I'd recommend as you pursue your passion.

Being free from financial constraint opens up a world of opportunity. The opportunity to draw whatever you choose on those white walls. The opportunity to make a difference.

The opportunity to truly live.

Frosting on the cake, indeed.

Learn from the Success of Others

If you look up the definition of "retire," you'll find "to withdraw from action or danger." In my mind, that's the exact opposite of what retirement should be. I prefer to think of it as "re-tire," an act in which we put new tires on our vehicles for the changing road conditions ahead. The beauty of "re-tire" is the reality that you can choose whatever tires you'd like and put them on whatever type of "car" you'd like to become in re-tirement. I'd go with big, wide mudders on a new 4x4 jeep, the best option to roam the mountains around our retirement cabin. For you, it may be nice summer radials on a Mercedes to give you a smooth and quiet ride down the highway ahead or racing slicks on a 1963 split-window Corvette.

⩵ RETIREMENT TIP 22 ⩵

Consider retirement as a time to re-tire
your chosen vehicle with new tires best
suited for the road ahead.

As you think about what kind of new tires you're putting on your car, it's worthwhile to have a look at what has been done by others who have been successful in figuring out how to re-tire with a purpose. For a case study on how to do it right, I'm highlighting someone near and dear to my heart. Let's look at my wife, Jackie, and a nonprofit she recently started called Freedom For Fido.

The Story of Freedom For Fido

Speaking from experience, I urge you to never underestimate the impact of retirement on a stay-at-home spouse or partner. In my case, my wife and I thought we were aligned on the whole retirement thing, until life threw us a curveball.

Three months after we made the decision to retire, Jackie's mom died.

Her mother's death taught us something. We had agreed Jackie would be a stay-at-home mom from the day our daughter was born in 1994. As our daughter finished high school and went off to college, Jackie's mom moved in with us. She was suffering from dementia and was no longer able to live on her own. My wife became her full-time caregiver for the next four years, at which point her mother moved into a nursing home. Jackie continued to visit her five or more days a week and took her role as caregiver seriously.

That all changed with her mother's passing, and my wife found herself a bit off-kilter. In hindsight, we've realized that Jackie's "job" was giving care to others and that her "job" had suddenly vanished. Unprepared for her own "retirement," she struggled to find a purpose. Mild depression set in, and we went through a few tough months. In her own words, "The feelings I had of being set adrift without a purpose were so unexpected."

One day she saw an episode of the Mike Rowe–hosted video series *Returning the Favor* in which he profiled a nonprofit in Oregon called Fences For Fido. The organization built free fences for low-income families who kept their dogs on a chain. A light went off for the lifelong dog lover. "I should do that HERE!" she said.

She took the first step. She contacted Fences For Fido and explained that she'd like to start a similar charity in the mountains of northern Georgia. With some guidance from the organization, she started walking down the path. Within a few months she had established a 501(c)(3) nonprofit, built a website (www.freedomforfido.com), put together a board of directors, and set up a bank account and post office box.

Three short months after taking that first small step, we were building our first fence. We haven't stopped since. The word has spread in our small mountain town, and the response has been overwhelming. Many people have contributed to the cause, and many others have helped on the fence builds. She recently gave a presentation to the board of directors of our local Humane Society, and they're talking about some partnership opportunities. She's got a tiger by the tail, and the tiger is starting to run.

More importantly, my wife has a purpose, and she's never been more energized. She's found her new tires. She's making a difference. She's having a ball. She was even profiled recently in a magazine article. She's being stretched beyond her comfort zone, and she's embracing the challenge with a smile on her face.

Look for ways to make a difference, to improve the lives of others.

Then take that first step. You'll be amazed where it can lead.

A Personal Challenge

Given the importance of passion in retirement, I'm going to end this book with a small personal challenge. I'll share a secret trick I've learned in the past five-plus years of blogging, and it's applicable to all areas in your life. In return for sharing this secret with you, I'm going to ask for something in return. I'm assigning you some homework. As a challenge, I encourage you to apply the concept I'm presenting in Retirement Tip 23 and then report back to me whenever you feel you've completed the assignment. Feel free to send me an e-mail at fritz@theretirementmanifesto.com to let me know what you've discovered.

═ RETIREMENT TIP 23 ═

If something interests you, pursue it.

Seems pretty simplistic, but like most things in life, it's a bit of an onion. Peel off a few layers, and that simple advice can get surprisingly complex. Your homework assignment is to create your personal case study on the topic of "Passion in Retirement." Let's assume the topic interests you and you decide to accept your assignment. A simple next step would be to Google the term and start reading through the results. In a matter of seconds, you'll have millions of results to work through. You've taken the first step. Go ahead and put the book down and dig into that rabbit hole for a while. Have some fun while you're at it.

Next, if you're not already a podcast listener, it's time to figure out how to do it. (Hint: Google it!) Once you've figured it out, I want you to look up "The Retirement Answer Man," hosted by Roger Whitney. Then scroll back through his archives and listen to all of his August 2019 episodes. He spent an entire month with experts on the topic of purpose and how to apply it to your retirement. I've listened to thousands of podcasts, and that series is among the best I've heard.

As a third step, your assignment requires some additional reading. Buy one or two books on the topic and subscribe to a few retirement blogs. I've included several book and blog recommendations in the resources sections (see page 115). Now that you have some time in retirement, I urge you to discover the love of reading.

Throughout the process, I want you to take some time to be introspective and think about what you're learning. Seek out opportunities to apply the concepts in your life. Start a journal, and write down the things that speak to you. You'll need that journal for your final assignment.

When you've completed the preceding steps, I encourage you to consider writing a 1,000-word article about what you've learned, how you've applied it in your retirement, and what the results have been. When you send me that e-mail, attach the document (preferably in Word or Google Docs format). At that point, your homework will be completed, and you'll be released for your summer vacation.

Assuming a few of you take the homework seriously, you can look for future posts on "The Retirement Manifesto" blog that have been written by the readers of this book. If you happen to be one of the readers who get their work published on my blog, you'll know you've received an "A+" on the assignment.

Somehow, that seems an appropriate way to conclude my first book.

≡ RETIREMENT TIP 24 ≡

Never stop learning. Cultivate your curiosity, and apply what you're learning.

The secret that I've learned over the past few years is that retirement is best lived with a positive attitude of curiosity, a willingness to explore, an openness to change. As you live your new life in retirement, continually seek out areas that interest you and apply the things you learn to your life.

Find something that interests you, and let serendipity set the course. Follow it as far as your curiosity leads, and then move on to the next.

Repeat. Repeat. Repeat.

Enjoy life.

THE KEY TAKEAWAYS FROM THIS BOOK

———o———

Throughout this book, I've sprinkled 24 tips on the keys to a successful retirement. These tips have been developed during my personal experience transitioning from a 33-year career in corporate America to a successful retirement in the Appalachian Mountains of northern Georgia. As I write these words, I have no way to know if these tips will work for you, but I trust there's some value in sharing my experience.

To summarize what I've learned on my journey, I've listed the 24 tips here. I encourage you to pick five of these tips and begin applying them in your life. I look forward to reading about their impact on your life when I receive your homework assignment. Thank you for taking the time to read this book, and I sincerely hope my work will help you achieve a great retirement.

1. Invest as much time as possible into planning for your retirement.
2. Focus on the type of life you want to live in retirement, and let that drive your list of required ingredients.

3. Spend time thinking about the nonfinancial in-gredients of your retirement. In time, you'll find they're more valuable than money.

4. Track your actual preretirement spending for a year, and then make adjustments based on your retirement lifestyle goals to get a firm estimate of your retirement spending requirements.

5. Build up cash reserves equal to two to three years of your spending prior to reaching retirement. This is the pool of cash you'll use to establish your retirement paycheck.

6. Consider setting up a "bucket system," whereby you allocate investments to one of three buckets based on how long it will be before you need to tap into the money.

7. If you're planning to downsize or relocate in re-tirement, spend extended time in your new location before you finalize your decision. Get involved in your new community while you're still working.

8. Plan to do any major spending required to create your ideal retirement while you're still working.

9. Don't wait until RMDs kick in at age 72 to ma-nage your pretax retirement savings. Consider "topping off" your tax bracket each year with withdrawals from your before-tax IRAs.

10. Take the time in your final weeks of work to say goodbye to your true friends at work. Your rela-tionships will change after retirement.

11. Your life in retirement will change with time. Realize that the initial euphoria will fade, and enjoy the transition to a longer-term approach to retirement that works for you.

12. Don't retire without thinking about how it's going to impact your relationships. You've never spent as much time together as you will in retirement. Plan for it.

13. Focus on developing "retirement relationships," ideally while you're still working.

14. Realize that the change resulting from retirement is as significant for a stay-at-home spouse or partner as it is for the one leaving the workplace. Take time prior to retirement to talk about your mutual expectations.

15. Take as much time as possible preparing for retirement while you're still working. It is the single biggest differentiator between success and struggle.

16. If you're struggling with your transition to retirement, don't hesitate to reach out for help. There are people who dedicate their lives to helping people. Let them help you.

17. Never stop learning. View technology as a means to personal growth, and seek out opportunities to continually learn in your retirement years.

18. Take the time to put the appropriate legal safeguards in place, and find a time to talk with your family about your wishes.

19. Rather than thinking about seeking your passion, ask yourself, "What can I do with my time that's important?" Committing your energy to something that matters to you is the true frosting on your retirement cake.
20. Throw as many things as possible against the wall, and see what sticks.
21. Seek to develop interests for all the spokes in your life. A wheel rolls best when the spokes are the same length.
22. Consider retirement as a time to re-tire your chosen vehicle with new tires best suited for the road ahead.
23. If something interests you, pursue it.
24. Never stop learning. Cultivate your curiosity, and apply what you're learning.

Retirement Resources

Retirement and Financial Websites

AARP: aarp.org—A comprehensive site whose mission is "to empower people to choose how they live as they age." With over 38 million members, this is a valuable resource for all retirees.

Certified Financial Planner Board of Standards: cfp.net—A licensing board for financial planners, with a mission to "benefit the public by granting the CFP certification." If you're looking for a financial planner to assist in your retirement planning, make sure they have the CFP certification.

Social Security Administration: ssa.gov—The site for managing everything related to your Social Security planning, with valuable online resources for your retirement planning. To see the annual report mentioned in this book, go to www.ssa.gov/oact/TRSUM/.

American Association of Individual Investors: aaii.com—A membership site for individual investors providing "unbiased, actionable investment education, information and research to help you grow your investment wealth."

Legal Zoom: legalzoom.com—A comprehensive online legal resource providing do-it-yourself will, living trust, and estate plan documents. Contact with lawyers available.

Nolo: nolo.com—A do-it-yourself legal site, with the option to connect with a lawyer in your area.

International Foundation of Employee Benefit Plans: ifebp.org—An online learning site with hundreds of classes available for a wide variety of retirement-related topics.

Personal Capital: personalcapital.com—A free online dashboard of your financial situation, including asset allocation, net worth, and a retirement calculator.

Health Insurance

Medicare: medicare.gov—The official U.S. government site for Medicare, with extensive resources on various Medicare options and plans.

Affordable Care Act: healthcare.gov—The official U.S. government site for health care plans provided by the Affordable Care Act.

Boomer Benefits: boomerbenefits.com—An independent expert repository for all things related to Medicare, including a free online introductory course to key Medicare issues.

Health Care Sharing Ministry Overview: en.wikipedia.org /wiki/Health_care_sharing_ministry—An overview of health care sharing ministry options. A few of the most common providers include:

- Christian Healthcare Ministries: chministries.org
- Liberty HealthShare: libertyhealthshare.org
- Christian Care Ministry Medi-Share: mychristiancare.org
- Samaritan Ministries: samaritanministries.org
- For additional details: wellkeptwallet.com /health-sharing-plans/

Health Markets: healthmarkets.com /local-health-insurance-agent/—Find a local health insurance agent among this database of more than 3,000 licensed agents.

Recommended Reading: Retirement Blogs

The growth of retirement blogs has become a valuable resource for people approaching retirement. Following is a list of some of my favorites, though it's far from exhaustive. Try some of the blogs listed or search online to find something that matches your particular situation.

The Retirement Manifesto: theretirementmanifesto.com (the author's blog)

Route to Retire: routetoretire.com

Think Save Retire: thinksaveretire.com

The White Coat Investor: whitecoatinvestor.com

Physician on FIRE: physicianonfire.com

Retire with Money Newsletter: money.com /newsletter/retire-with-money/

Early Retirement Now: earlyretirementnow.com

Nerd's Eye View: kitces.com

Retirement Researcher: retirementresearcher.com

Financial Independence Hub: findependencehub.com

The Balance: thebalance.com

Financial Samurai: financialsamurai.com

Freedom Is Groovy: freedomisgroovy.com

Intentional Retirement: intentionalretirement.com

Retire Hoppy: retirehoppy.com

Make Smarter Decisions: makesmarterdecisions.com

Women Who Money: womenwhomoney.com

Four Pillar Freedom: fourpillarfreedom.com

Get Rich Slowly: getrichslowly.org

New Retirement: newretirement.com

Can I Retire Yet: caniretireyet.com

Jillian Johnsrud: jillianjohnsrud.com

Best Wallet Hacks: wallethacks.com

Sensible Money: sensiblemoney.com

Recommended Reading: Retirement/Finance Books

Anspach, Dana. *Control Your Retirement Destiny: Achieving Financial Security Before the Big Transition.* Fort Collins, CO: A Book's Mind, 2016.

Astor, Bart. *Roadmap for the Rest of Your Life: Smart Choices About Money, Health, Work, Lifestyle—and Pursuing Your Dreams.* Waterville, ME: Thorndike Press, 2013.

Collins, JL *The Simple Path to Wealth: Your Road Map to Financial Independence and a Rich, Free Life.* CreateSpace, 2016.

Drak, Mike, Rob Morrison, and Jonathan Chevreau. *Victory Lap Retirement: Work While You Play, Play While You Work.* Oakville, Ontario: Milner & Associates, Inc., 2019.

Ellis, Charles D., Alicia Haydock Munnell, and Andrew Eschtruth. *Falling Short: The Coming Retirement Crisis and What to Do About It.* New York, NY: Oxford University Press, 2014.

Kirkpatrick, Darrow. *Can I Retire Yet?: How to Make the Biggest Financial Decision of the Rest of Your Life.* Chattanooga, TN: Structure By Design, 2016.

Kirkpatrick, Darrow. *Retiring Sooner: How to Accelerate Your Financial Independence.* Chattanooga, TN: Structure By Design, 2013.

Mamula, Chris, Brad Barrett, and Jonathan Mendonsa. *Choose FI: Your Blueprint to Financial Independence.* Glen Allen, VA: ChooseFI Media, 2019.

Pfau, Wade D. *Safety-First Retirement Planning: An Integrated Approach for a Worry-Free Retirement.* Vienna, VA: Retirement Researcher Media, 2019.

Ruffenach, Glenn, and Kelly Greene. *The Wall Street Journal Complete Retirement Guidebook: How to Plan It, Live It, and Enjoy It.* New York, NY: Three Rivers Press, 2007.

Stein, J. David. *Money for the Rest of Us: 10 Questions to Master Successful Investing.* New York, NY: McGraw Hill, 2019.

Vernon, Steven G. *Money for Life: Turn Your IRA and 401(k) into a Lifetime Retirement Paycheck.* Oxnard, CA: Rest-of-Life Communications, 2012.

Whitney, Roger. *Rock Retirement: A Simple Guide to Help You Take Control and Be More Optimistic About the Future.* New York, NY: Morgan James Publishing, 2018.

Recommended Listening: Retirement Podcasts

It is reported that only 5 percent of Baby Boomers listen to podcasts, and the 95 percent who don't are missing out on a valuable resource for their retirement planning. Following are some of the most relevant podcasts for people approaching retirement. I've listened to all of them, and I've appeared as a guest on most of them as well. For links to the shows I've appeared on, see the "About" tab on my website (theretirementmanifesto.com/about).

If you've not yet discovered podcasts, I strongly encourage you to pick several from the list and give them a try.

New Retirement: newretirement.com

The Retirement Answer Man: rogerwhitney.com

Retirement Starts Today Radio: retirementstarts todayradio.com

The Retirement Wisdom Podcast: retirementwisdom.com /retirement-podcast

ChooseFI: choosefi.com

DoughRoller: doughroller.net

Stacking Benjamins: stackingbenjamins.com

Your Money, Your Wealth: purefinancial.com/ymyw

Radical Personal Finance: radicalpersonalfinance.com

Better Money Decisions: bettermoneydecisions .com/podcast

Sound Retirement Radio: soundretirementradio.com

The Money Guy Show: moneyguy.com

Retire Hoppy: retirehoppy.com

Money for the Rest of Us: moneyfortherestofus.com

Where to Find a Certified Financial Planner

Paladin Registry: paladinregistry.com—A free service that matches you with prescreened financial fiduciaries.

Certified Financial Planner Board of Standards: cfp.net—An online database of licensed CFP professionals.

Heritage Wealth Planning: heritagewealthplanning.com—Josh Scandlen

New Retirement: newretirement.com—Steve Chen

The Retirement Answer Man: rogerwhitney.com—Roger Whitney

Finding Your Passion Resources

Web Resources: Personal Support

SAMHSA: samhsa.gov—The U.S. government's Substance Abuse and Mental Health Administration. Call (800) 662-HELP (800-622-4357).

Better Help: betterhelp.com—Affordable, private online counseling utilizing licensed, professional therapists. Rated the top online Christian counseling service in 2019.

Alcoholics Anonymous: aa.org

HelpGuide: helpguide.org—An online mental health resource providing empowering, evidence-based information that you can use to help yourself or your loved one.

Mental Help America: mhanational.org—A nonprofit dedicated to promoting mental health.

eCounseling.com: e-counseling.com—An online resource with a variety of counseling resources and local references.

National Suicide Prevention Lifeline: (800) 273-TALK (8255)

Help.org: help.org—An online resource to find local counselors, including a veteran support line (www.help.org /substance-abuse-rehab-for-veterans/).

Psychology Today: psychologytoday.com—A comprehensive site with an online directory for psychologists in your area.

Web Resources: Purpose

Encore: encore.org—"Second acts for the greater good."

Clearer Thinking: clearerthinking.org—Mini-courses to help you understand yourself. Its Lifetime Aspirations tool will help you explore the essences of "meaning" and "purpose."

Age Wave: agewave.com—The nation's thought leader on issues related to an aging population.

Retirement Quotes on Purpose: wow4u.com/retirement

Simon Sinek: simonsinek.com/find-your-why—An interactive course that helps you find your "why."

Getting Through: gettingthru.org/holistic—A nonprofit organization with courses designed to accelerate your personal growth.

Just Between Us: justbetweenus.org—A Christian site with extensive content on finding your purpose in life.

Recommended Reading: Purpose

Brooks, David. *The Second Mountain: The Quest for a Moral Life*. New York, NY: Random House, 2019.

Bstan-'dzin-Rgya-Mtsho, Dalai Lama XIV, and Howard C. Cutler. *The Art of Happiness: A Handbook for Living*. New York, NY: Riverhead Books, 2009.

Buettner, Dan. *Blue Zones: 9 Lessons for Living Longer from the People Who've Lived the Longest*. Washington, DC: National Geographic, 2012.

Buford, Bob. *Halftime: Moving from Success to Significance*. Grand Rapids, MI: Zondervan, 2015.

Clear, James. *Atomic Habits: Tiny Changes, Remarkable Results: An Easy & Proven Way to Build Good Habits & Break Bad Ones*. New York, NY: Avery, 2018.

Crowley, Chris, and Henry S. Lodge. *Younger Next Year: Live Strong, Fit and Sexy Until You're 80 and Beyond*. New York, NY: Workman Publishing, 2007.

Drak, Mike, Rob Morrison, and Jonathan Chevreau. *Victory Lap Retirement: Work While You Play, Play While You Work*. Oakville, Ontario: Milner & Associates, Inc., 2019.

Dyer, Wayne. *The Shift: Taking Your Life from Ambition to Meaning*. Carlsbad, CA: Hay House, 2010.

Farrell, Chris. *Purpose and a Paycheck: Finding Meaning, Money and Happiness in the Second Half of Life*. New York, NY: HarperCollins Leadership, 2019.

Frankl, Viktor E. *Man's Search for Meaning: An Introduction to Logotherapy*. Boston, MA: Beacon Press, 2006.

Freedman, Marc. *How to Live Forever: The Enduring Power of Connecting the Generations.* New York, NY: Public Affairs, 2018.

Goff, Bob. *Love Does: Discover a Secretly Incredible Life in an Ordinary World.* Nashville, TN: Thomas Nelson Publishers, 2015.

Guillebeau, Chris. *The Happiness of Pursuit: Find the Quest That Will Bring Purpose to Your Life.* London: Pan Books, 2017.

Hobbs, Charles. *Time Power.* New York, NY: Harper & Rowe, 2007.

Laura, Robert. *Naked Retirement: Living a Happy, Healthy & Connected Retirement.* Retirement Project, 2014.

Leider, Richard, and Alan Webber. *Life Reimagined: Discovering Your New Life Possibilities.* San Francisco, CA: Berrett-Koehler Publishers, Inc., 2013.

Rohr, Richard. *Falling Upward: A Spirituality for the Two Halves of Life.* San Francisco, CA: Jossey-Bass, 2011.

Sedlar, Jeri, and Rick Miners. *Don't Retire, REWIRE!: 5 Steps to Fulfilling Work That Fuels Your Passion, Suits Your Personality, and Fills Your Pockets.* New York, NY: Alpha, 2018.

Smith, Hyrum W. *Purposeful Retirement: How to Bring Happiness and Meaning to Your Retirement.* Coral Gables, FL: Mango Publishing, 2017.

Tolle, Eckhart. *A New Earth: Awakening to Your Life's Purpose.* New York, NY: Penguin Publishing, 2008.

Recommended Blogs and Podcasts: Purpose

BLOGS

Mark Manson: markmanson.net

Some Kind of 50: somekindof50.com

Sightings Over Sixty: sightingsat60.blogspot.com

Lifehack: lifehack.org

Raptitude: raptitude.com

Next Avenue: nextavenue.org

Alixandra Foisy: alixandrafoisy.com/blog/

PODCASTS

Retirement Wisdom: retirementwisdom.com

Rock Your Retirement: rockyourretirement.com

The Retirement Answer Man: rogerwhitney.com

Good Life Project: goodlifeproject.com

Inspire Nation: inspirenationshow.com

Where to Find a Retirement Coach

International Coach Federation: coachfederation.org

Retirement Options: retirementoptions.com

Life Coach Hub: lifecoachhub.com/retirement-coach

Noomii—The Professional Coach Directory: noomii.com /retirement-coaches

Retirement Wisdom: retirementwisdom.com—Joe Casey started as an executive coach but expanded into retirement coaching due to the growing demand from his clients.

Jack Canfield Coaching: jackcanfield.com

Charities/Volunteer Opportunities/ Activities

CASA GAL: nationalcasagal.org—Advocate for children who have experienced neglect or abuse.

Habitat for Humanity: habitat.org—Help build homes for those in need.

Senior Corps: nationalservice.gov/programs /senior-corps—An easy way to find senior volunteering opportunities online.

National Parks Volunteer: nps.gov/getinvolved /volunteer.htm—Join the VIP program.

Musicians on Call: musiciansoncall.org—Bring the joy of music to a health care facility.

AARP Foundation Experience Corps: aarp.org /experience-corps/

Team Rubicon: teamrubiconusa.org—Veterans helping with disaster relief.

CoolWorks: coolworks.com—Get a seasonal job in a national park or anywhere else.

Meetup: meetup.com—Find activities and clubs in your area.

Road Scholar: roadscholar.org—Volunteer while you travel.

Global Volunteers: globalvolunteers.org—Community service projects with a purpose.

Peace Corps: peacecorps.gov—The Peace Corps has a specific program for those over 50.

Big Brothers Big Sisters of America: bbbs.org—Make a difference in a young person's life.

Meals on Wheels: mealsonwheelsamerica.org—Help seniors age with dignity.

American Red Cross: redcross.org—Your local Red Cross needs you.

IRS: irs.gov/individuals/irs-tax-volunteers—Volunteer income tax assistance.

Rotary Club: rotary.org

Kiwanis: kiwanis.org

Online Educational Opportunities

Coursera: coursera.org

Udemy: udemy.com

Khan Academy: khanacademy.org

TEDEd: ed.ted.com

Codecademy: codecademy.com

Stanford Online: online.stanford.edu

Road Scholar: roadscholar.org—This site's motto says it all: "Whatever you're interested in, we have the learning adventure for you." A focus on travel education.

Index

H

Health care spending, 16–17,
23–24, 82–83
Health Care Sharing Ministries
(HCSMs), 83
Hobbs, Charles, 101–102
Housing, 32–36

I

Identity, loss of, 71–73
Incapacitation, 88–90
Interests, pursuit of, 106–108
Investments, 3

J

Joint Trusts with Rights of
Survivorship (JTWROS), 90

K

Koontz, Dean, 1

L

Legal documents, 88–91
Leider, Richard J., 71
Lifestyle needs, 11
Living wills, 89

M

Medical insurance, 16–17, 23–24,
82–83
Mental stimulation, 10
Money. *See* Finances

O

One Retirement Question project,
94–97

P

Passions, 13–14, 77, 94–97
Pensions, 15–17
Personal growth, 84
Planning stage
determining type of retirement life,
2–6, 99–100
financial calculations, 6–9, 20–21,
24–27
importance of, 66–67, 75–76
nonfinancial considerations, 9–12
process, 12–14
Possibilities, 45
Power of attorney (POA), 89
Pretax savings, 38–41
Purpose, finding, 13–14, 77, 94–97

R

Reaching out, 78–81
Regrets, 97
Relationships
with coworkers, 46, 55–56
developing new, 56–58
with significant others, 54–55, 60–63
Relocating, 32–34
Required Minimum Distributions
(RMDs), 38–41, 86
"Retirement Activity Jar," 71
Retirement tips, 110–113
"Re-tiring," 103–104
Revenue Act (1978), 15
Roiphe, Anne, 73

Routines, 49, 52–53
Rubbo, Joe, 80–81

S

"Safe Withdrawal Rate" (SWR), 25–26
Schedules, 78
SECURE Act (2019), 39
Social connections, 11, 56, 76
Social Security, 85–86
Spirituality, 11–12, 77
Struggling, 78–81

T

Taxes, 24, 38–41
Technology, 83–85
"Test Retirement," 98–99
Timing, of retirement, 13
Tips, 110–113
"Toy spending," 34–36
Transitions, 4, 49–50, 75–76

U

"UnRetirement," 103

V

Victory Lap Retirement (**Drak, Morrison, and Chevreau**), 103

W

Ware, Bronnie, 97

Webber, Alan M., 71
Weil, Andrew, 76
Whitney, Roger, 107
Wills, 88–90
Wolpert, Ed, 57
Working, in retirement, 8

Acknowledgments

In my years of writing at The Retirement Manifesto, I've learned that writing must be about the reader. Words only have an impact if they're read and applied in a person's life, and the real joy of writing comes when you see that words you've written are making an impact. Therefore, my first acknowledgment is to the reader. You've motivated me with your positive response to my words and have helped turn writing into a passion. Thank you for helping me to discover this passion—it's made my retirement better than I could have imagined.

Second, I believe that life is better when shared with a person you love. I've been blessed with a wife I don't deserve. Jackie's been there for me through 33 years of corporate work, and her support throughout my life has been beyond compare. Sharing the retirement of our dreams together has been one of the main keys to my happiness, and I can't imagine life without her. Thank you for your love, Jackie.

Third, this book would not have been possible without the professionals at Rockridge Press and Callisto Media. To Joe, for seeking me out. To Marisa, for your positive encouragement and support as these words were being written. To the entire team, for your professionalism in finalizing this book.

Finally, a special thanks to God. There's nothing more important than the assurance of an eternal life—without God's sacrifice, it's a gift none of us would know. For that, I am eternally grateful. As you're seeking passion in your retirement, don't overlook the spiritual aspects of life. They matter more than anything here on earth. Finally, a verse that has motivated me to share my gift of writing:

"Each one should use whatever gift he has received to serve others, faithfully administering God's grace in its various forms."
—1 Peter 4:10

About the Author

 Fritz Gilbert retired after more than three decades in corporate America, where he progressed through the various levels of a multinational corporation serving the global aluminum industry. His award-winning blog "The Retirement Manifesto" is focused on helping people achieve a great retirement. Fritz and his wife, Jackie, live in a cabin in Blue Ridge, Georgia, an Appalachian mountain town where they're active in their local church and various local charities, including Jackie's charity Freedom For Fido (FreedomForFido.com).

When he's not writing, Fritz enjoys spending his time outdoors and is an avid fly fisherman, mountain biker, hiker, camper, photographer, and fitness fanatic. He also cherishes his daily walks in the woods with their four dogs, who run the household. Fritz and Jackie also travel cross-country in their RV to visit their daughter and her family in the Pacific Northwest. Find Fritz on Twitter (@RetireManifesto), Facebook (The Retirement Manifesto), and Instagram (@The_Retirement_Manifesto), or drop him an e-mail at fritz@theretirementmanifesto.com.